TOTES AMAZE!

25 bags to make for every occasion

AMANDA McKITTRICK

hardie grant books

MELBOURNE · LONDON

CONTENTS

PROJECTS

INTRODUCTION

Next time you step out, take a look around and you'll see people carrying totes of all shapes, sizes and styles. A simple bag, the humble tote has risen from the plain calico sack to a highly adaptable fashion statement. The combinations of fabric, lining and handles are endless, and each bag can be as unique as the individual.

Pretty or practical, or a combination of both, there's a tote for all occasions. Whether you are a fashionista, a hip art student, or an environmentally conscious shopper, *Totes Amaze* will inspire you to create a bag that suits your style and taste.

Inside this book you'll find a selection of simple and achievable tote bag projects for crafters of all skill levels, with simple instructions, templates and illustrations to guide you.

The totes are not limited to the specific purposes suggested in the book; you'll find that many of the designs will suit various needs. Use the gardening tote as a beach bag, for example. It's easy to add additional pockets or other features to the existing designs. And you don't need years of sewing experience – the simple techniques and designs in this book will allow you to easily create and customise your own tote.

Whip up a basic tote, or spend some time crafting one for a special occasion, gift or specific purpose. Let your imagination run free and be adventurous with your fabric choices – you'll totes amaze your friends and passers-by alike.

GETTING STARTED

GETTING STARTED

ABOUT THE INSTRUCTIONS

The instructions are divided into simple steps for making the bag, lining, straps or handles, and finally assembling the bag. Not all bags have pockets and closures but these can easily be added, if you wish, by following the instructions later on in this introductory text. If you choose to customise the lining of your bag, consider all the things you carry with you and how you'd like them to be organised.

Pattern pieces

If the instructions mention pattern pieces, refer to the pattern sheet at the back of the book. You can either trace patterns onto a separate sheet of paper, or simply cut along the lines of the pattern sheet supplied.

Corner pattern pieces should be placed on the raw edges of the rectangular/square piece of fabric. Simply trace the shape onto the fabric and cut along that line.

Some pattern pieces will need to be cut on the fold of the fabric. Fold the fabric along the straight grain, parallel to the selvedge. Place the pattern on the fold of the fabric as indicated, and cut through all layers. Transfer over markings for darts or magnetic snaps at this point too.

The right and the wrong sides of the fabric are indicated in the instructional illustrations: the right (patterned) side of the fabric is shaded; the wrong (unpatterned) side of the fabric is blank.

Most of these totes are made using basic rectangles of fabric, which should be cut on the straight grain where possible. The seam allowance on all edges is 1 cm (⅜ in), unless this is indicated otherwise.

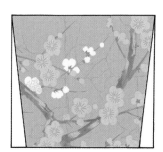

Corner pattern pieces

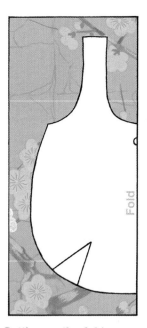

Cutting on the fold

SEWING KIT

- Tailor's chalk, dressmaker's pencil or disappearing ink marker pen – to make temporary marks on fabric, so that you know where to cut, hem or make darts

- Dressmaker's scissors – reserve these for cutting fabric only, as cutting paper blunts the scissors

- Paper-cutting scissors – keep a separate pair of scissors on hand for cutting paper

- Pinking shears – great for cutting edges with a decorative zigzag effect; edges cut with pinking shears are also less prone to fraying

- Measuring tape – a retractable one is handy

- Pins

- Safety pins – have a few different sizes; large ones can be used for threading elastic through casings

- Iron and ironing board

- Cotton pressing cloth – to place over fabrics to protect them while they're being ironed; a clean white handkerchief or even some baking paper will work

- Sewing needles – most hand-sewing needles (sharps) range in size from 1 to 10 (the larger the number, the finer the needle); use fine needles for fine fabrics and thicker needles for thick fabrics

- Sewing thread – for most projects, a cotton-polyester blend thread will work well

- Sewing machine and needles – you don't need a high-tech sewing machine: one that does straight stitch, zigzag stitch and buttonholes will get you a very long way

- Seam ripper or unpicker – for easily unpicking stitching mistakes

- Ruler – for accurately marking seams and darts

STITCH GUIDE

Straight stitch

The most basic stitch, used for seams and hems. You can vary the stitch length according to what you are sewing. In general, use a shorter stitch length for finer fabrics and a longer stitch length for thicker or heavy fabrics.

Zigzag stitch

A saw-toothed stitch that is great for finishing raw edges. The length and width of the stitches can be adjusted. Use a narrower zigzag on fine fabrics and a wider one on heavy fabrics.

Topstitch

A permanent running stitch worked along the edge of the project on the right side of the fabric. It helps the edge to lie flat, and can also be used for decorative purposes. For machine topstitching, use a small to medium straight stitch.

Back stitch

This stitch is used to secure each end of your sewing, preventing the stitches from unravelling. Sew a few stitches, reverse stitch over these, then continue sewing. Repeat at the end of the line of stitching to secure the other end.

Basting stitch

A long stitch used to temporarily join two or more layers of fabric together. The stitches are usually removed once the permanent seam is sewn, so they don't need to be particularly neat or even. Use the longest straight stitch length on your sewing machine.

FABRIC AND INTERFACING

Selecting fabric

With so many fabrics on offer, it's sometimes hard to choose. Finding the right bag fabric can either be an immediate 'must-have' experience, or an exercise in frustration as you pace up and down the aisles of your local store hunting for that perfect print.

There's no golden rule or great secret to finding the perfect fabric, just keep an open mind and follow your instincts when it comes to colour and print choices. I tend to look for the bag fabric first and then find a lining that complements this choice.

Consider the bag shape and size when hunting for fabrics: a large pattern will look best on a large bag; likewise, a small pattern will look best on a smaller bag.

Cotton, denim, canvas and upholstery fabrics are best for bags (avoid stretch or delicate fabrics). Your local fabric store should have a decent selection of these fabrics, but if not, then online shopping is a great option. If you do decide to buy fabric from an online seller, keep in mind that the colours on the screen might display differently to the actual fabric. This isn't always necessarily disappointing – I have been pleasantly surprised in the past when opening my delivery to discover prints more beautiful than expected. Because you can't physically pick up and feel the fabric, it's also wise to take note of the fabric weight and type when ordering online. If you have any doubts, simply email the seller and they will be only too happy to assist.

Most fabrics come in a standard roll width of 115 cm (45¼ in). Almost all of the projects in this book therefore specify fabric of this width in the materials list.

Don't forget to buy thread that best matches your new fabric while you're at it, as there's nothing more frustrating than starting on your project only to discover you don't have thread to suit (I've made this mistake more than once!).

Directional patterns

Some fabrics have a directional pattern (the print has an obvious 'right way up'), while others have a non-directional pattern (the print is the same in every direction). When working with directional patterns, make sure you check that the print is facing the right way up before you cut and sew. Also note that if a tote is made from a single piece of fabric folded in half and your fabric has a directional pattern, the print will be upside down on one side of the bag.

Quick tips for working with Mexican oilcloth

Most projects in this book call for cotton fabric, but there are a few that use oilcloth. Oilcloth is a brightly coloured, boldly designed fabric that has the benefit of being waterproof and very easy to clean.

Mexican oilcloth can be awkward to work with at first, but with a little patience and some testing on a scrap piece before you start work on your project, you'll be on your way.

- Loosen the tension on your sewing machine.

- Use a leather needle.

- Use either strong 100 per cent polyester or a cotton-polyester blend thread.

- Don't use pins, as they'll leave permanent holes – instead, use sticky tape to hold your pieces in place as you sew.

- If the oilcloth is creased, lay it in the sun for a while to soften the cloth, then smooth the creases out. You can place a towel over the cloth and run an iron over the towel to smooth creases too – just be sure not to iron directly on the oilcloth, as it will melt!

- Test-sew on a scrap piece of oilcloth before you start on your project.

Interfacing

Interfacing is applied to the wrong side of the fabric and provides reinforcement, stiffening or shaping to your work. It is available in fusible or sew-in forms, in various thicknesses, and in white, grey or black – the one you choose will depend on your project. For example, a lighter interfacing would be more suited to a heavy fabric, so the final bag isn't too stiff; likewise, a lightweight cotton will have more structure when a heavier interfacing is used.

I prefer to use sew-in interfacing when making bags, as fusible (iron-on) interfacing can sometimes give an uneven 'bubbled' effect, either immediately or after a period of time. Sew-in interfacing solves this problem.

If you do opt for fusible interfacing, always test it with a scrap of fabric before proceeding with the project, to ensure an appropriate match. Never iron fusible interfacing with the sticky side up, as it will stick to your iron.

SEAMS, EDGES AND HEMS

Seam (seam line)

The seam is the line of stitching joining two pieces of fabric.

Seam allowance

The seam allowance is the margin of fabric outside the final stitched seam line. I have used a 1 cm (⅜ in) seam allowance for these projects, unless otherwise mentioned.

Finishing raw edges

It's important to finish the edges of the fabric before sewing or hemming, to stop the fabric from fraying and to achieve a clean and professional look. There are a couple of ways to do this: either zigzag stitch with your sewing machine or overlock the raw edge of the fabric.

Double hem

A double hem gives a nice finish to the project by hiding the raw edge of the fabric. Simply turn the raw edge over at least 5 mm (¼ in), then turn it over again according to the project instructions and stitch down.

Single hem

If the fabric is thick, a double hem will be too bulky, so opt instead to overlock or zigzag the raw edge, then fold it over once and sew it down.

SHAPING: DARTS, PLEATS, GATHERS, CURVES AND CORNERS

Darts

Darts create shape and volume in a bag so it doesn't look too flat.

How to sew a dart

1 To easily transfer dart markings from the pattern sheet to the fabric, first pin the pattern piece to the wrong side of your fabric. Cut along one dart line on the pattern and fold it over along the other line. Draw a line onto the fabric along the cut edge and the folded edge.

2 On the wrong side of the fabric, match up the two dart lines on the edge of the fabric so the fold meets the centre point of the dart. Press the fold flat with your finger.

3 Pin in place and stitch from the edge inwards to the end of the line, then, instead of backstitching, tie the two thread ends into a knot where the stitching ends.

4 Press the dart flat towards the outer edge of the fabric piece.

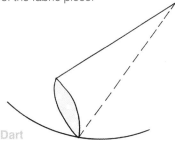

Dart

Pleats

Pleats are folds in the fabric that gather in large amounts of fabric without adding bulk. Pleats are generally not stitched down all the way along their length.

How to sew pleats

1 Fold and press the fabric as indicated in the instructions to create the pleats.

2 Pin the pleats down, press, and baste in place.

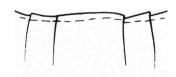

Pleats

Gathers

Gathers give a more relaxed look compared with pleats and darts, yet still serve the purpose of gathering in large amounts of fabric.

How to sew a gathered edge

1 Set your sewing machine to the longest stitch length and sew two rows of stitching about 5 mm (¼ in) apart, close to the edge of the fabric. Don't backstitch to secure the thread, and leave a length of thread at each end of the rows of stitching.

2 Taking hold of the bobbin thread only, gently pull the ends of each thread, gathering the fabric evenly as you draw it up.

3 When you are satisfied with the look of the gathering, tie both ends of the threads in a small knot.

Gathers

Clipping curves

Clipping an inward-facing curved seam reduces bulk and allows the fabric to sit flat, giving the seams some ease. Make small cuts perpendicular to the seam along the edge of the curve – but don't cut into the stitching, or you'll have to sew a new seam around it or replace the piece entirely!

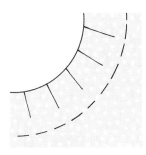

Clipping a curve

Notching curves

Cutting notches into an outward-facing curved seam reduces bulk and allows the fabric to sit flat. Cut little, evenly spaced triangles along the seam line, taking care not to cut through the stitching.

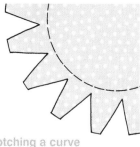

Trimming corners

Trimming excess fabric from corners allows the fabric to sit flat. Trim with care to avoid cutting into the stitching.

Trimming a corner

Boxed corners

Boxed corners are an easy way to create a flat base for your tote. With just a few simple steps, you can add dimension and structure to any sized bag.

How to sew boxed corners

1 Take your bag (or lining) and, with the wrong side of the fabric facing out, pinch the fabric at each side of one corner and carefully match up the side seam with the bottom seam. Measure in from the corner point as indicated in the instructions, and draw a line across the corner at this mark to make a triangle.

2 Pin the corner in place and stitch along this line, backstitching at each end.

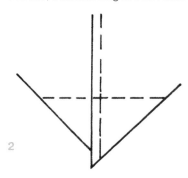

3 Cut off the corner triangle approximately 1 cm (⅜ in) from the line of stitching. Finish off the raw edges.

HARDWARE AND HANDLES

Zippers

Zippers are available in a wide variety of styles and lengths. The zipper sizes required for the projects in this book are specified; however, as a rule, choose one that is slightly longer than you need and either trim it down to size or tuck the excess down into the bag. To trim a zipper, stitch across the teeth by hand at the desired length and snip off the end if the teeth aren't metal.

Magnetic snaps

Magnetic snaps are small fasteners for bags that add a clean, professional finish and are very easy to install. They consist of four parts: two magnetic discs that snap together and two metal support pieces (washers) that are placed over the prongs at the back of the snap. They are available in different sizes, so choose one that suits your bag design: for example, if you are making a small bag, select a small snap. Avoid using magnetic snaps on phone and computer bags, just in case.

How to install a magnetic snap

1 Trace the pattern marking where indicated onto the wrong side of each lining piece (or measure the centre point on each lining piece and mark it).

2 Cut two small squares of fusible interfacing and iron one over each of these marked points. This will provide support to the fabric where it's pulled by the snap.

3 With a marker pen, trace the metal support piece onto the square of interfacing and cut the two slits for the prongs.

4 Insert one side of the magnetic snap through the slits from the right side of the fabric. Place the metal support piece over the prongs and fold the prongs over to the inside of the circle.

5 Iron another small square of interfacing over the back of the secured snap.

6 Attach the other half of the magnetic snap to the other lining piece using the same process.

D-rings and O-rings

D-rings and O-rings are, as their names suggest, 'D' and 'O' shaped attachments that connect a bag strap or handle to the bag. They are available in different materials and sizes. Choose a size and style to suit your bag design. These rings are both functional and decorative.

Handles and straps

The fun part of making bags is selecting the handles. With so many choices on offer, you're sure to find some that reflect your own personal style. Etsy and eBay are goldmines for unique designs, and your local craft store should have a selection of webbing in different thicknesses.

Webbing is great for the humble tote; it's easy to work with and is available in a variety of widths and colours. Reinforce webbing and fabric straps once stitched to your tote by sewing a square across the width of the webbing, with an 'X' through the centre of it.

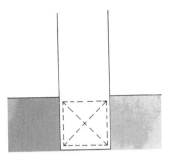

Attaching webbing

Leather handles will add a professional touch to your tote and are very easy to attach. Some are available with fixed rings and other embellishments, or ready-made holes for stitching the handles to the fabric of your bag or for attaching with rivets.

Many other handle styles are available, such as chain, bamboo, and frames for wide openings.

Making your own fabric handles or straps is another way of enhancing your design – you can control the length and width, and select a fabric that complements or contrasts with your design. Adding D-rings, O-rings or metal sliders can add an extra bit of pizazz and give your bag a professional finish.

How to make fabric handles/straps

1 Fold each strap piece in half lengthwise, with right sides facing together, and stitch 5 mm (¼ in) from the raw edge.

2 Press the seam open, then turn the strap right side out. (A safety pin attached to one end will make feeding the fabric through a lot easier.)

3 Press the strap flat, with the seam centred.

4 On each strap, stitch a seam 1 cm (⅜ in) in from each side along the entire length.

4

POCKETS

How to create an internal zippered pocket

1 Select a zipper size and cut a rectangle of fabric slightly wider than the length of the zipper and as high as you like (depending on the height of the bag and how deep you want the pocket) – bear in mind that the pocket piece will be folded up in half when finished. For example, my zipper length is 20 cm (8 in) and my rectangle of fabric is 23 cm (9 in) wide x 32 cm (12½ in) high. When folded and stitched, my pocket will measure 21 cm (8¼ in) wide x 13 cm (5 in) deep – the final depth being half the height minus 3 cm (1¼ in) for seam allowance.

2 With the lining facing right side up, place the pocket piece on top with wrong side up. Position the top of the pocket piece 7.5 cm (3 in) from the top edge of the lining. Match the centre of the pocket piece to the centre of the lining (the easiest way to do this is to mark the centre on both pieces and match up the marks). Pin in place.

3 Draw a rectangle onto the pocket piece measuring 1.5 cm (⅝ in) x 18 cm (7 in) – i.e. the zip length minus 2 cm (¾ in). To do this, measure 1 cm (⅜ in) and 2.5 cm (1 in) from the top of the pocket piece and draw two lines across at these points. Now mark 9 cm (3½ in) either side of the centre of the pocket, and draw in the sides of the rectangle.

4 Stitch along all sides of the rectangle.

5 Draw a line across the middle of this rectangle, stopping 5 mm (¼ in) from each end. Cut a slit along this line (cutting through both layers of fabric), then cut two angled slits at each end, making sure you don't cut through the stitching.

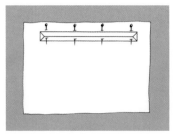

5

6 Push the entire pocket piece through the newly created hole, so the wrong sides of the pocket and lining are now facing, and press all edges down flat.

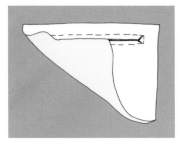

6a

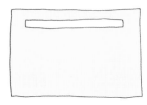

6b

7 Turn the lining piece over so that the right side is facing up and the pocket piece is on the back. Position the zipper in the hole and pin down. Don't worry if the zipper is longer than the hole, it can be cut down to size later.

8 Stitch around all four sides of the rectangle to secure the zipper. Keep the stitching close to the edges of the rectangle and make sure the pocket fabric doesn't get caught up in your stitching at the back.

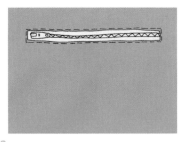

8

9 Turn the lining over to the wrong side again and fold up the pocket piece in half, right sides facing, and pin. Stitch around all four sides, making sure you don't catch the lining fabric in the stitching. And that's it! A cute little zippered pocket in your lining.

How to create a slip pocket

There are two ways to do this: one uses a double layer of fabric for a stronger pocket, the other a simple hem. Both techniques are used in projects in this book – you can choose which you prefer for additional pockets.

Hemmed edge pocket

1 Cut one piece of pocket fabric to size.

2 Zigzag stitch or overlock the raw edges.

3 Fold the two sides and one longer edge over 5 mm (¼ in) to the wrong side of the fabric and press in place.

4 Fold the remaining long edge over 1 cm (⅜ in) and press, then fold over another 1 cm (⅜ in) and press again. This will be the top edge of the pocket.

5 Stitch along the folded edge, close to the fold.

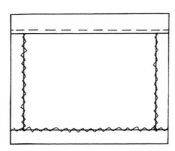

5

Double layer pocket

1 Cut one piece of pocket fabric to size.

2 Fold the pocket piece in half with right sides facing and press.

3 Stitch along all three open sides, leaving a 4 cm (1½ in) opening on the top edge for turning.

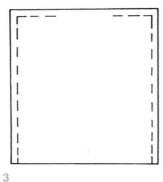

3

4 Turn right side out, stitch up the opening, and press flat. Topstitch close to the top edge of the pocket.

Attaching a slip pocket

1 Position the pocket on the bag or lining piece and pin in place.

2 Stitch along the sides and across the bottom, close to the edge. Don't stitch the pocket opening closed!

EMBELLISHMENTS

Making your own bias binding

Bias binding makers are nifty little gadgets, allowing you to easily make bias binding to match your bag fabric. Preparation can sometimes be time consuming, but it's worth it for a professional, individual look.

Bias binding makers come in different sizes, but I find a 12 mm (½ in) binding maker is useful for a range of projects. Cut strips of fabric at double the width of the finished binding. For example, for a finished width of 12 mm (½ in), cut strips 2.5 cm (1 in) wide.

How to make bias strips and binding

1 Cut the fabric across from one selvedge edge to the other.

2 Fold the cut edge diagonally across so that it lines up against the selvedge.

3 Cut along the diagonal fold – this will be your starting point for marking up the strips.

4 Measure widths of 2.5 cm (1 in) from the diagonal cut edge, marking the lines using a ruler and tailor's chalk or a disappearing ink marker pen.

5 Cut along these lines.

6 If the strips are too short, stitch two (or more) together at the ends.

7 If you don't have a bias binding maker, skip this step. If you do have one, feed the strip evenly through the widest end of the binding maker and watch as the binding appears nicely folded on the other side. Press flat as you go.

8 If you don't have a bias binding maker, fold over the long edges of the strip to meet in the centre, pressing flat as you work your way along.

How to apply bias binding

Bias binding can seem a little daunting at first, but once you've mastered it you'll never look back. It gives a clean finish by encasing raw edges, and lies flat and smooth around curves. Bias binding can be sewn on to the right or wrong side of the fabric for different effects. You don't need to neaten the raw edge of your fabric before applying bias binding (although you can if you want to).

1 Open out one folded edge of the binding, and fold one end over about 2.5 cm (1 in) to the wrong side (this will create a neat join later). Match up the raw edge of the fabric with the unfolded (raw) edge of the binding, right sides facing. Pin or baste in place.

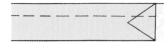

1

2 Sew along the fold of the binding, starting at the folded end and leaving a tail of 2.5 cm (1 in) at the other end.

3 Fold the binding over to the wrong side of the fabric and press in place with your fingers (shaping it to the curve if there is one). Sew along the very edge of the binding.

4 Repeat this process for remaining edges, allowing an overlap of 2.5 cm (1 in) where the ends of the binding meet. Cut the binding end at an angle (to reduce bulk), tuck it under and sew down.

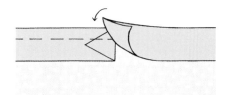

4

Tassels

Tassels are a flirty, fun way to add that little bit of quirk to your tote, and they are so easy to make. Use embroidery thread or thin yarn for best results.

How to make tassels

1 Decide how long you want your tassels to be and cut a rectangle of card of the same height to wrap the thread around.

2 Wrap thread around the piece of card until it is as fat as you would like your tassel to be.

2

3 Use a needle to insert a long length of thread through the top loops of the wound thread and tie tightly in a knot to secure the threads.

4 Pull the wound thread off the card and cut the loops at the bottom.

4

5 Holding onto the ends of the thread you tied, shape the tassel. Wrap a piece of thread around the top to create the tassel neck.

6 Trim the ends of the tassel to neaten, and attach to your tote using the thread at the top.

6

Pompoms

Pompoms are wonderfully tactile embellishments that take no time to fluff up. Combine with tassels for double the goodness.

How to make pompoms

1 Wrap yarn around two or three of your fingers until it's nice and fat.

2 Feed a strand of yarn through the middle of the wound threads and tie it tight.

2

3 Pull the yarn off your fingers and cut the loops at each end.

3

4 Fluff up the pop-pom, trim off any straggly bits, and attach to your tote using the thread at the top.

PROJECTS

LIBRARY TOTE

Libraries may be places of quiet, but there are no rules when it comes to library bags! Make a statement next time you visit the library with a loud splash of colour and bold design.

This tote has two rows of stitching along each edge, not only to reinforce the seams for heavy loads, but as a decorative touch. (As a bonus, those pesky raw edges will be hidden.) Use contrasting thread to highlight this stitching if you dare.

The tote is made from one piece of fabric folded in half, so I would recommend choosing fabric that has a non-directional pattern, or is plain or textured.

Materials

Medium–heavy weight cotton fabric: approx. 80 cm (31½ in) wide x 120 cm (47¼ in) high

LIBRARY TOTE

FINISHED SIZE

▷ 42 cm (16½ in) wide x 44 cm (17¼ in) high

CUT

◁ 1 x bag piece: 44 cm (17¼ in) wide x 49 cm (19¼ in) long, cut on the fold – so the opened piece measures 44 cm (17¼ in) wide x 98 cm (38½ in) long

◁ 2 x strap pieces: 12 cm (4¾ in) x 63 cm (24¾ in)

SEW

Straps

▷ **1** Fold each strap piece in half lengthwise, with right sides facing together, and stitch 1 cm (⅜ in) from the raw edge.

◁ **2** Press the seam open, then turn the strap right side out. (A safety pin attached to one end will make feeding the fabric through a lot easier.)

▷ **3** Press the strap flat, with the seam centred. Stitch a seam 5 mm (¼ in) in from each edge along the entire length.

3

◁ **4** Fold the bag piece in half, right sides facing together. Fold over the top edge 2 cm (¾ in) to the wrong side on both sides, and press.

▷ **5** On the folded edge on each side of the bag, position the strap 9.5 cm (3¾ in) from the raw side edges and pin. Make sure the straps aren't twisted, then stitch in place.

◁ **6** Fold the top edge over 2 cm (¾ in) to the wrong side of the bag, then fold the strap up over this hem and pin in place.

◁ **7** Run two lines of stitching along this folded edge, 5 mm (¼ in) from the top and bottom of the folded hem, to secure the hem and straps in place.

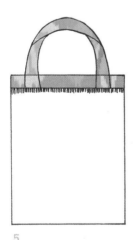

5

Bag

1 With right sides still facing, pin the raw side edges of the bag piece together.

2 Stitch 5 mm (¼ in) from the edge along both sides. Press the seam to one side – don't press the seam open!

3 Turn the bag right side out and press flat.

4 Topstitch 5 mm (¼ in) from the edge along both sides and across the bottom. Then topstitch again, this time 1.5 cm (⅝ in) from the edge.

4

MARKET TOTE

Brighten up your early morning trip to the market with a quick and easy lined tote. It's large enough to bag up some fresh fruit and veg, but not so big that it's a struggle to carry. Add some colourful handles and you'll be the envy of all those shoppers carrying their plain old green bags.

I used strawberry-shaped leather stitch-on handles for this tote. A wide variety of handles can be found online on sites such as Etsy, with so much choice you're bound to find the perfect handles for your bag.

Choose a lightweight plastic or waterproof lining if you want to protect your bag from water and dirt, or go with a bright highlight colour to add a bit of fun to your shopping.

Materials

- Medium weight cotton fabric for bag: approx. 115 cm (45¼ in) wide x 65 cm (25½ in) long
- Light–medium weight cotton fabric for lining: approx. 115 cm (45¼ in) wide x 65 cm (25½ in) long
- Heavy weight interfacing: approx. 115 cm (45¼ in) wide x 65 cm (25½ in) high – if you can't find long interfacing at your local craft store, use two layers of medium weight interfacing
- Stitch-on handles

MARKET TOTE

FINISHED SIZE

▶ 46 cm (18 in) wide x 36 cm (14¼ in) high

CUT

▶ 2 x bag pieces: 49 cm (19¼ in) wide x 44 cm (17¼ in) long

▶ 2 x lining pieces: 49 cm (19¼ in) wide x 44 cm (17¼ in) long

▶ 2 x interfacing pieces: 49 cm (19¼ in) x 44 cm (17¼ in)

SEW

Bag

▶ **1** Place the bag pieces together with right sides facing. Sandwich the bag pieces between the two pieces of interfacing. Pin all layers together. Stitch 1.5 cm (⅝ in) from the edge along both sides and across the bottom edge.

▶ **2** To create boxed corners, follow the instructions on page 14, measuring 6 cm (2⅜ in) from the corner point. Turn the bag right side out.

Lining

▶ **1** Pin the lining pieces together with right sides facing. Stitch 1.5 cm (⅝ in) from the edge along both sides and across the bottom, leaving a 15 cm (6 in) opening on one side for turning the bag right side out later on.

▶ **2** Create boxed corners for the lining, as in step 2 for sewing the bag.

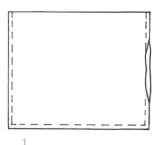

1

Assemble

▷ **1** On the right side of the bag, position the ends of the first handle at least 2 cm (¾ in) from the top edge of the bag (keeping in mind you'll need 1.5 cm (⅝ in) for seam allowance) and as far from each side edge as is appropriate for your chosen handles – make note of this measurement for attaching the handle to the other side of the bag. Stitch the handles on through all layers on each side.

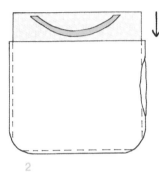

2

▷ **2** With the bag right side out and the handles folded down to the outside of the bag, insert the bag into the lining (which should still be wrong side out).

▷ **3** Pin the top raw edges of the bag and lining together. Stitch all the way around the top, 1.5 cm (⅝ in) from the edge.

▷ **4** Pull the bag through the opening in the lining, then stitch the hole closed and push the lining down into the bag.

▷ **5** Press the bag, using a light cotton pressing cloth to protect your fabric and handles from the hot iron.

▷ **6** Topstitch around the top edge of the bag, close to the fold.

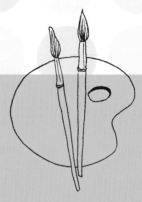

ART TOTE

As a creative type, you'll be only too familiar with the many bits and pieces you need to carry about. Making a tote to suit your creative needs is simpler than you might think. A few layers of padding will help to keep your tools of the trade safe from harm.

This tote is large enough to carry your sketchbook and has two internal pockets – one large enough for a tablet, the other for smaller items such as a pencil case, wallet or phone. If you need more pockets, just cut another pocket piece for the other side of the bag and repeat the same process to attach it.

Materials

- Medium weight cotton fabric for bag: approx. 115 cm (45¼ in) wide x 120 cm (47¼ in) long
- Cotton fabric for lining and pocket: approx. 115 cm (45¼ in) wide x 2 m (2¼ yd) long
- Medium weight interfacing: approx. 115 cm (45¼ in) wide x 120 cm (47¼ in) long
- Medium weight batting: approx. 115 cm (45¼ in) wide x 2 m (2¼ yd) long
- 3.8 cm (1½ in) webbing for straps: 140 cm (55 in) long

ART TOTE

FINISHED SIZE

- 41 cm (16¼ in) wide x 46 cm (18 in) high

CUT

- 2 x bag pieces: 44 cm (17¼ in) wide x 49 cm (19¼ in) long
- 2 x lining pieces: 44 cm (17¼ in) wide x 49 cm (19¼ in) long
- 2 x interfacing pieces: 44 cm (17¼ in) x 49 cm (19¼ in)
- 2 x batting pieces for bag: 44 cm (17¼ in) x 49 cm (19¼ in)
- 1 x pocket piece: 44 cm (17¼ in) wide x 68 cm (26¾ in) long
- 1 x batting piece for pocket: 44 cm (17¼ in) x 34 cm (13½ in)
- 2 x webbing straps: 70 cm (27½ in) long

SEW

Bag

1 Place the bag pieces together with right sides facing. Sandwich the bag pieces between two pieces of interfacing and then between two pieces of batting. Pin all layers together. Stitch along both sides and across the bottom, 1.5 cm (⅝ in) from the edge. Turn right side out.

2 On both sides of the bag, pin the webbing straps 6.5 cm (2½ in) from the top edge and 8 cm (3 in) in from each side. Turn the cut edges of the straps under 5 mm (¼ in) to stop fraying, or seal the ends with fray-stop. Make sure the straps aren't twisted. Stitch on the straps by sewing a square across the width of the webbing, with an 'X' through the centre of it to provide reinforcement.

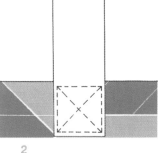

2

Lining and pocket

1 Fold the pocket fabric in half with wrong sides facing and sandwich the batting between the two layers of fabric. Sew a line of stitching close to the folded edge.

2 Position the pocket on top of one piece of the lining fabric with right side facing up, and pin the raw side and bottom edges together. Measure 28 cm (11 in) across from one edge and mark a vertical line. Sew along this line to divide the pocket in two.

3 Place the other piece of lining on top, right sides facing, and pin. Stitch along both sides and across the bottom, 1.5 cm (⅝ in) from the edge, leaving a 15 cm (6 in) opening on one side for turning.

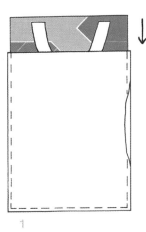

Assemble

1 With the bag right side out and the handles folded down to the outside of the bag, insert the bag into the lining (which should still be wrong side out).

2 Pin the top raw edges of the bag and lining together. Stitch all the way around the top edge.

3 Pull the bag through the opening in the lining, then stitch the hole closed and push the lining down into the bag.

4 Press the bag, using a light cotton pressing cloth to protect your fabric and straps from the hot iron.

5 Topstitch around the top edge of the bag, close to the fold.

SPARE PAIR OF SHOES TOTE

Whether you're a busy executive working in the city, a dancer on your way to class, or someone who just likes to swap shoes during the day, This tote is the perfect way to transport your alternative pair of shoes in style.

Make the tote from a washable fabric, and be sure to wash and dry the fabric before sewing to avoid future shrinkage.

A drawstring top closes the bag and this can be folded down inside so the bag can be used as a regular tote. Versatility, style and a spare pair of shoes…what girl doesn't need this tote?

Materials

- Medium–heavy weight washable cotton fabric for bag: approx. 115 cm (45¼ in) wide x 50 cm (19¾ in) long
- Light–medium weight fabric for lining and drawstring top: approx. 115 cm (45¼ in) wide x 90 cm (1 yd) long
- 2.5 cm (1 in) webbing for straps: 125 cm (49¼ in) long
- Drawstring cord or ribbon: 80 cm (31½ in) long
- Cord stopper (suited to the thickness of the cord/ribbon)

SPARE PAIR OF SHOES TOTE

FINISHED SIZE

- 35 cm (13¾ in) wide x 40 cm (15¾ in) high

CUT

- 2 x bag pieces: 37 cm (14½ in) wide x 42 cm (16½ in) long
- 2 x lining pieces: 37 cm (14½ in) wide x 42 cm (16½ in) long
- 2 x drawstring top pieces: 37 cm (14½ in) wide x 22 cm (8⅜ in) long
- 2 x webbing straps: 62 cm (24½ in) long

SEW

Bag

1 Pin the bag pieces together with right sides facing. Stitch along both sides and across the bottom.

2 Turn the bag right side out and press flat.

Lining

1 Pin the lining pieces together with right sides facing. Stitch 1.5 cm (⅝ in) from the edge along both sides and across the bottom, leaving a 15 cm (6 in) opening on one side for turning the bag right side out later on.

Drawstring top

1 On both drawstring top pieces, zigzag stitch or overlock the shorter raw edges.

2 Pin these two pieces together with right sides facing and mark the fabric 6.5 cm (2½ in) from the top edge on each side.

3 Starting from this mark, stitch down each side. Press the seams open.

4 To create the casing for the cord, fold over the top edge 1 cm (⅜ in) to the wrong side of the fabric and press. Fold over another 2.5 cm (1 in) and press again. Stitch the casing down, sewing 5 mm (¼ in) in from the folded edges.

3

4

Assemble

1 On both sides of the bag, pin the webbing straps 6 cm (2⅜ in) from the top and 8 cm (3 in) in from each side. Turn the ends of the webbing under 1 cm (⅜ in) to prevent fraying. Stitch along the edges of the webbing and close to the top of the bag to secure the straps in place

2 With the straps folded down towards the bottom of the bag, position the drawstring top piece over the top of the bag with right sides facing. Match up the raw edges – the casing should be facing towards the bottom of the bag. Pin in place.

3 With the bag right side out and the lining still wrong side out, insert the bag into the lining.

4 Pin all three edges together at the top of the bag and sew all the way around the top edge.

5 Pull the bag through the opening in the lining, then stitch the hole closed and push the lining down into the bag.

6 Press the top edge flat, then topstitch all the way around through all layers, 5 mm (¼ in) from the edge.

7 Thread the cord or ribbon through the casing, using a safety pin attached to one end to help you pull it through.

8 Feed the cord through the cord stopper and tie knots in the end of the cord.

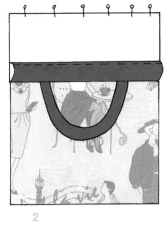

2

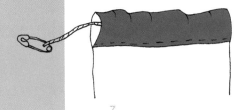

7

SIX-POCKET GARDENING TOTE

There are many items we need when out in the garden: seeds, gloves, trowel, hat and insect repellent, to name a few. With this sturdy six-pocket tote you'll be ready to head out to the vegetable patch with all the necessities at hand.

This tote is not limited to use in the garden of course; it's large enough to be used as a beach bag, craft bag or whenever you need a large, strong bag with ample storage.

Materials

- Medium–heavy weight cotton fabric for bag: approx. 115 cm (45¼ in) wide x 70 cm (27½ in) long
- Light–medium weight fabric for lining: approx. 115 cm (45¼ in) wide x 70 cm (27½ in) long
- Hessian (burlap) or heavy-weight fabric for pockets: approx. 115 cm (45¼ in) wide x 80 cm (31½ in) long
- 3 cm (1¼ in) webbing for straps: 320 cm (3½ yd) long
- Sturdy plastic for the base: 12 cm (4¾ in) x 34 cm (13½ in) – available at art and craft supply stores

SIX-POCKET GARDENING TOTE

FINISHED SIZE

▶ 45 cm (17¾ in) wide x 42 cm (16½ in) high

CUT

▶ 2 x bag pieces: 48 cm (19 in) wide x 51 cm (20 in) long

◢ 2 x lining pieces: 48 cm (19 in) wide x 51 cm (20 in) long

▶ 2 x pocket pieces: 48 cm (19 in) wide x 61 cm (24 in) long

◢ 2 x webbing straps: 160 cm (63 in) long

SEW

Pockets

▶ **1** Fold the two pocket pieces in half lengthwise, so they measure 30.5 cm (12 in) high x 48 cm (19 in) wide. Press.

2 With right sides of the bag and pocket pieces facing up, pin the pocket pieces to the bag pieces, making sure the bottom raw edges are aligned.

Straps

◢ **1** On the right side of both bag pieces, position the webbing straps 13 cm (5 in) in from each side, aligning the ends of the straps with the bottom raw edge of the bag. Pin in place. Secure to the bag by stitching close to the edge along each side of the strap, sewing from the bottom to the top and stopping 2.5 cm (1 in) from the top edge of the bag. Stitch a square across the width of the webbing at the top of the strap, with an 'X' through the centre of it to provide reinforcement (see page 15).

Bag

▶ **1** Pin the bag pieces together with right sides facing. Stitch along both sides and across the bottom.

▶ **2** To create the boxed corners, follow the instructions on page 14, measuring 6 cm (2⅜ in) from the corner point. Turn the bag right side out.

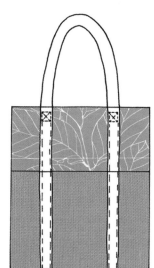

1

3 Place the plastic piece in the base of the bag.

Lining

1 Pin the lining pieces together with right sides facing. Stitch along both sides and across the bottom, leaving a 15 cm (6 in) opening on one side for turning the bag right side out later on.

2 Create boxed corners for the lining, as in step 2 for sewing the bag.

Assemble

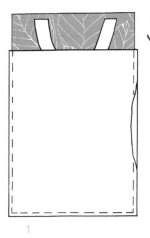

1

1 With the bag right side out and the straps folded down to the outside of the bag, insert the bag into the lining (which should still be wrong side out).

2 Pin the top raw edges of the bag and lining together. Stitch all the way around the top edge.

3 Pull the bag through the opening in the lining, then stitch the hole closed and push the lining down into the bag.

4 Press the bag, using a light cotton pressing cloth to protect your fabric and straps from the hot iron.

5 Topstitch around the top edge of the bag, close to the folded edge.

POCKET SHOPPER TOTE

The Pocket Shopper is the perfect little tote to tuck away in your handbag in preparation for those unexpected shopping trips.

This lightweight bag folds up into a small square, so it won't weigh you down and won't take up much space in your handbag. As a bonus, the pocket that the tote is stored in can double as a pocket for your keys, purse or sunglasses when the bag is in use.

Materials

Light weight cotton fabric for bag: approx. 115 cm (45¼ in) wide x 60 cm (23½ in) long

Pocket fabric: 30 cm (12 in) wide x 50 cm (19¾ in) long

2.5 cm (1 in) wide cotton webbing for straps: 130 cm (51¼ in) long

Shopping List

POCKET SHOPPER TOTE

FINISHED SIZE

- Bag: 39 cm (15⅜ in) x 39 cm (15⅜ in)
- Folded into pocket: 14 cm (5½ in) x 14 cm (5½ in)

CUT

- 2 x bag pieces: 42 cm (16½ in) wide x 42 cm (16½ in) long
- 1 x pocket piece: 17 cm wide (6¾ in) x 32 cm (12½ in) long
- 2 x webbing straps: 65 cm (25½ in) long

SEW

Pocket

1 Fold the pocket piece in half with right sides facing, so that the folded piece measures 16 cm (6¼ in) x 17 cm (6¾ in). Press.

2 To make the double layer pocket, follow the instructions on page 18.

3 Select a bag piece to be the front of the bag and position the pocket on the right side of the fabric, 13.5 cm (5⅜ in) in from each side and the bottom. Pin in place.

4 Attach the pocket to the bag piece, sewing along both sides and across the bottom, stitching close to the edges of the pocket. Don't stitch the pocket opening closed!

Bag

1 Place the remaining bag piece on top of the first, right sides together, and pin. Sew along both sides and across the bottom. Zigzag stitch or overlock the raw edges.

2 Fold over the top edge of the bag 1 cm (⅜ in) to the wrong side of the fabric and press, then fold over another 1 cm (⅜ in) and press again.

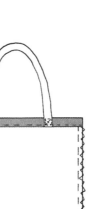

5

3 Position the straps 10 cm (4 in) in from each side of the bag on the folded top edge, turning the raw ends under 1 cm (³⁄₈ in) to prevent fraying. Pin in place.

4 Stitch across the top edge of the bag, close to the fold line of the hem, stopping to remove the pins as you reach the straps.

5 Stitch a square across the width of the webbing at the end of each strap, with an 'X' through the centre of it to provide reinforcement (see page 15).

6 Turn the tote right side out and press flat.

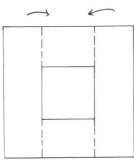

7a

7 To store, fold each of the four sides in, then push the bag into the pocket as you turn it inside out.

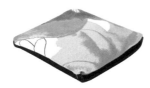

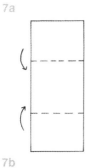

7b

TINY TOTS TOTE

A tiny tote for the tiny tots. This cute bag is perfect for kids to carry their favourite small toys or trinkets in.

This tote uses a tiny amount of fabric, so it's a great project if you have some bright fabric scraps lying around. I designed the bag with girls in mind, but you could easily adapt it for a boy: simply replace the two handles with one long strap, leave off the pompom edge, and select fabrics more suited to your boy.

Enlarge the pattern piece to make an adult-sized tote if you wish – the same instructions apply.

Materials

Cotton fabric for bag: approx. 40 cm (15¾ in) wide x 40 cm (15¾ in) long

Cotton fabric for lining: approx. 40 cm (15¾ in) wide x 40 cm (15¾ in) long

Cotton fabric for handles: approx. 20 cm (8 in) wide x 50 cm (19¾ in) long

Pompom/bobble edging: 1 m (39 in)

Tiny Tots Tote pattern piece

TINY TOTS TOTE

FINISHED SIZE

- 20 cm (8 in) wide x 24 cm (9½ in) high

CUT

- 2 x bag pieces: cut on the fold from pattern piece
- 2 x lining pieces: cut on the fold from pattern piece
- 2 x handle pieces: 32 cm (12½ in) long x 6 cm (2⅜ in) wide

SEW

Bag

1 Lay one bag piece right side up and arrange the pompom trim around the edge, with the bobbles facing in. Baste in place, aligning the edge of the trim with the raw edge of the fabric.

2 Place the remaining bag piece right side down on top and pin the edges together. Stitch around the curved edges, then carefully notch the curves (see page 14). Turn the bag right side out.

Lining

1 Pin the lining pieces together with right sides facing. Stitch around the curved edges, leaving a 4 cm (1½ in) opening in the bottom for turning the bag right side out.

2 Notch the curves.

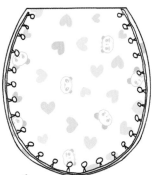

1

Handles

1 To make the handles, follow the instructions on page 15 (steps 1–3 only).

2 On each handle, stitch a seam 3 mm (⅛ in) in from each side along the entire length.

Assemble

1 Turn the lining right side out. On both sides of the lining, position the handles 1.5 cm (⅝ in) in from each side edge, aligning the raw edges and making sure the handles are facing down to the bottom of the bag and are not twisted. Stitch them on, about 5 mm (¼ in) in from the top edge.

2 Turn the lining wrong side out again. With the bag facing right side out, insert it into the lining, making sure that the handles are facing down towards the bottom of the bag.

3 Pin the top raw edges of the bag and lining together. Stitch all the way around the top edge.

4 Pull the bag through the opening in the lining, then stitch the hole closed and push the lining down into the bag.

5 Press the top edge of the bag flat and topstitch close to the seam.

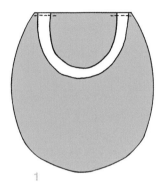

1

CLASSIC CARRYALL
TOTE

The Classic Carryall Tote features a zippered top, ring handles and an external pocket. Make the pocket in a highlighting fabric against a plain bag fabric for a striking effect. Choose handles with rings attached – there is a wide assortment of leather styles available online. Alternatively, make your own fabric handles (see page 15) from coordinating fabric and attach them using separate O-rings (fold the fabric through the ring and stitch to secure).

Materials

- Medium–heavy weight cotton or canvas for bag: approx. 60 cm (23½ in) wide x 100 cm (39 in) long
- Cotton fabric for lining: approx. 60 cm (23½ in) wide x 100 cm (39 in) long
- Cotton fabric for straps: approx. 30 cm (12 in) wide x 100 cm (39 in) long
- Fabric for front pocket: approx. 30 cm (12 in) wide x 70 cm (27½ in) long

- Interfacing: approx. 60 cm (23⅝ in) wide x 100 cm (39 in) long
- Handles with O-rings attached (bought or homemade)
- Zipper: 40 cm (15¾ in) long
- Cardboard or hard plastic: 8 cm (3 in) x 31 cm (12¼ in)

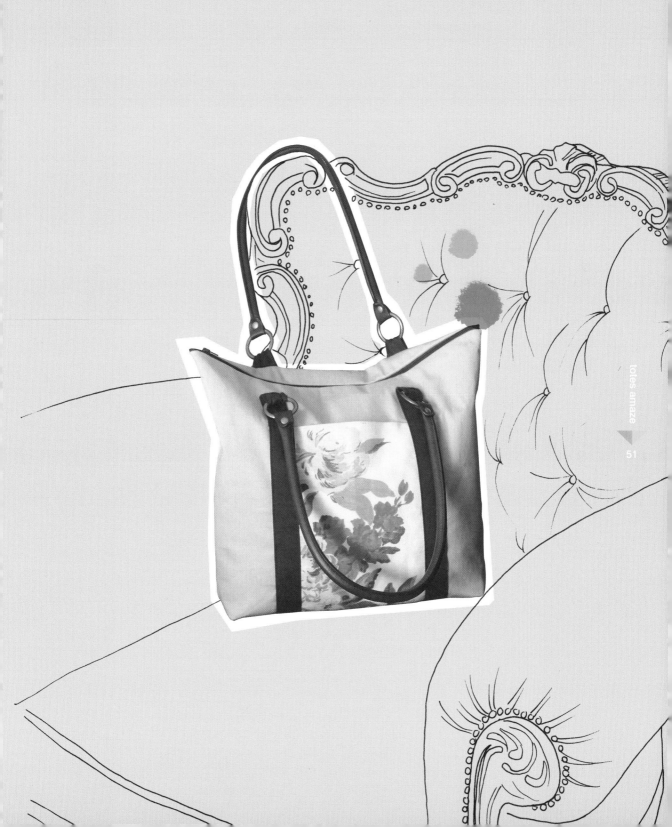

CLASSIC CARRYALL TOTE

FINISHED SIZE

▶ 39 cm (15⅜ in) wide x 32 cm (12½ in) long

CUT

▶ 1 x bag piece: 42 cm (16½ in) wide x 76 cm (30 in) long

◢ 1 x lining piece: 42 cm (16½ in) wide x 76 cm (30 in) long

▶ 1 x interfacing piece: 42 cm (16½ in) wide x 76 cm (30 in) long

◢ 1 x pocket piece: 20 cm (8 in) wide x 56 cm (22 in) long

◢ 2 x strap pieces: 7 cm (2¾ in) wide x 76 cm (30 in) long

SEW

Pocket

▶ **1** Fold the pocket piece in half with right sides facing together, so it measures 20 cm (8 in) x 28 cm (11 in). Stitch along the short raw edge. Turn right side out and press flat.

Straps

▶ **1** Fold each strap piece in half lengthwise with right sides facing together, and stitch 5 mm (¼ in) from the raw edge.

◢ **2** Press the seam open, and turn the strap right side out. (A safety pin attached to one end will make feeding the fabric through a lot easier.)

◢ **3** Press the strap flat, with the seam centred.

Bag

▶ **1** Baste the interfacing piece to the wrong side of the bag piece.

▶ **2** Fold the bag piece in half with right side out so that it measures 42 cm (16½ in) wide x 38 cm (15 in) high. Line up the stitched edge of the pocket piece with the bottom (folded) edge of the bag, 11 cm (4⅜ in) in from each side. Pin in place through the top layer of bag fabric and interfacing only.

3 Open out the bag piece and lay it right side up. Position the straps over the side edges of the pocket, covering the raw edges, and pin in place. Stitch along both edges of each strap, stopping 5 cm (2 in) from the top and bottom of the bag piece. Stitch a line across each strap at this point.

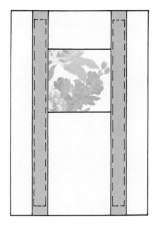

3

4 Insert the O-rings of the handles over the ends of the straps, fold the strap ends under and stitch through all layers to secure.

4

5 Fold the bag piece in half with right sides facing and handles folded down into the bag, and stitch along the sides.

6 To create the boxed corners, follow the instructions on page xx, measuring 4 cm (1½ in) from the corner point.

Lining

1 Fold the lining piece in half with right sides facing. Stitch along the sides.

2 Create boxed corners for the lining, as in step 6 for sewing the bag.

Assemble

1 With the bag right side out, insert the cardboard or plastic piece into the base of the bag. Insert the lining (still wrong side out) into the bag. Pin the top raw edges together.

2 Zigzag stitch or overlock all the way around the top edge.

3 Turn the bag inside out so the lining is facing out.

4 Position the zipper so it lines up with the side edges of your bag (cut to size if necessary). Pin one edge of the zipper to the top edge of the bag, right sides facing, and stitch 1 cm (⅜ in) from the edge.

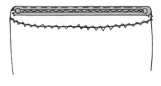

4

5 Open the zipper, then pin and stitch the other side of the zipper to the other side of the bag.

6 Turn the bag right side out. Topstitch along both sides of the zipper, 5 mm (¼ in) in from the seam.

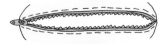

6

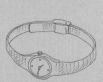

TIME SAVER TOTE

Need a quick and easy tote to complement your outfit? Looking for the perfect project for that scrap fabric you've had lying around for months? This tote is for the girl on the run, the girl with a sense of style but limited time, or the girl who feels a little intimidated by complex craft projects. It's easy, cute and achievable in next to no time – and the possibilities for fabric and handle combinations are endless. Dust off that sewing machine and whip up a one-of-a-kind Time Saver Tote.

Choose heavier fabric for a sturdier bag, or lighter fabric for a tote you can fold up and keep in your handbag for unexpected shopping trips.

Materials

- Cotton or fabric of your choice for bag: approx. 115 cm (45¼ in) wide x 70 cm (27½ in) long
- Cotton webbing or ribbon for straps: 120 cm (47¼ in) long

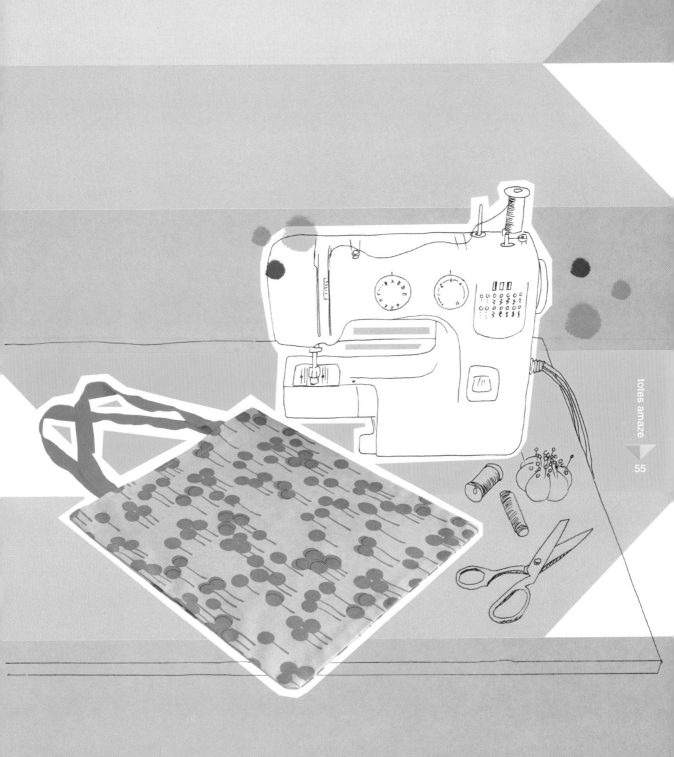

TIME SAVER TOTE

FINISHED SIZE

▲ 35 cm (13¾ in) wide x 40.5 cm (16 in) high

CUT

▲ 2 x bag pieces: 38 cm (15 in) wide x 47 cm (18½ in) high

◢ 2 x webbing straps: 60 cm (23⅝ in) long

SEW

Bag

▲ **1** On the top edge of each bag piece, with fabric facing right side up, position the straps 6.5 cm (2½ in) in from each side of the bag, aligning the raw edges and making sure the handles are facing down to the bottom of the bag piece. Ensure the handles are not twisted.

◢ **2** Stitch the ends of the straps in place, sewing close to the top edge of the fabric.

◤ **3** Turn the top edge of each bag piece over 1.5 cm (⅝ in) to the wrong side of the fabric and press, then turn over another 2.5 cm (1 in) and press again. Pin in place, with handles facing up towards the top of the bag piece.

▲ **4** Stitch across the top edge of each bag piece, 5 mm (¼ in) from the folded edge of the hem, to secure the hem and straps in place. Stitch another row across, 5 mm (¼ in) from the top edge of the bag piece.

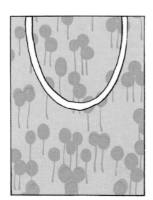

1

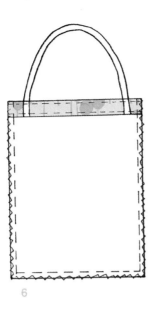

6

5 Pin the two bag pieces together with right sides facing. Stitch 1.5 cm (⅝ in) in from the edge along both sides and across the bottom.

6 Zigzag stitch or overlock these three raw edges.

7 Turn the bag right side out and press flat.

JUMBO BEACH TOTE

Water resistant and extra large so you can carry towels, swimming costumes and sunscreen, the beach tote is the perfect fuss-free bag for those gloriously warm summer days. Make it in an eye-popping choice of Mexican oilcloth and you're set to dazzle on your day out at the beach.

The beauty of oilcloth is that it is very low maintenance – simply wipe clean if it gets dirty. As an added bonus, it doesn't fray, so no hemming or lining is required. (Before you start cutting or sewing, refer to the tips for working with Mexican oilcloth on page 11.)

I finished the edges of this tote and the straps with pinking shears, but if you prefer, you can fold the edges over and hem them, finish them with bias binding, or just leave them as they are.

Materials

- Oilcloth: approx. 120 cm (47¼ in) wide x 100 cm (39 in) long
- Pinking shears (if you want zigzag edges)
- Adhesive tape (to use instead of pins)

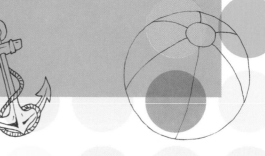

JUMBO BEACH TOTE

FINISHED SIZE

- 49 cm (19¼ in) wide x 42 cm (16½ in) high

CUT

- 2 x bag pieces: 52 cm (20½ in) wide x 53 cm (21 in) long
- 4 x strap pieces: 4 cm (1½ in) wide x 66 cm (26 in) long

SEW

Bag

1 Trim the top edge of both bag pieces with pinking shears if you want a zigzag edge.

2 Place the bag pieces together with right sides facing and secure with pieces of adhesive tape around each edge.

3 Stitch 1.5 cm (⅝ in) from the edge along both sides and across the bottom.

4 To create boxed corners, follow the instructions on page 14, measuring 8 cm (3 in) from the corner point.

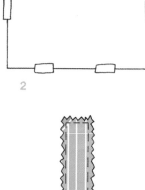

2

Straps

1 For each strap, place two strap pieces together with wrong sides facing and secure along the length with small pieces of adhesive tape.

2 Sew along each side, 1 cm (⅜ in) from the edge.

3 Trim the edges of the straps with pinking shears if desired.

3

Assemble

1 Turn the bag right side out. Position the straps on the outside of the bag, 5 cm (2 in) from the top edge and 10 cm (4 in) in from each side, securing them with adhesive tape.

2 Stitch the straps to the bag by sewing a rectangle across the width of each strap, with an 'X' through the centre of it to provide reinforcement (see page 15).

TWO-TONE TOTE

Two fabrics combine to create a tote that is stylish and very practical. Choose contrasting or complementary fabrics, patterned or plain, to create your own unique Two-tone Tote.

This basic tote is large and lined, without a closure, but you can add pockets and a zipper or magnetic snap if you like (see instructions on page 15).

Materials

Cotton fabric for top panel of bag: approx. 115 cm (45¼ in) wide x 40 cm (15¾ in) long

Cotton fabric for bottom panel of bag and base: approx. 115 cm (45¼ in) wide x 40 cm (15¾ in) long

Cotton fabric for lining: approx. 115 cm (45¼ in) wide x 70 cm (27½ in) long

Cotton fabric for straps: approx. 115 cm (45¼ in) wide x 40 cm (15¾ in) long

Interfacing: approx. 115 cm (45¼ in) wide x 70 cm (27½ in) long – if your fabric is light weight, choose a thicker interfacing; if it's heavier weight, use a lighter weight interfacing

Two-tone Tote pattern pieces: corner for top panel; corner for bottom panel; corner for lining; bag base

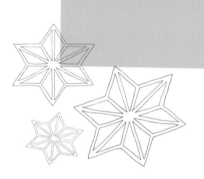

TWO-TONE TOTE

FINISHED SIZE

▶ 52 cm (20½ in) wide x 34 cm (13⅜ in) high

CUT

* Refer to the instructions on page 8 for placing and cutting corner pieces.

◢ 2 x top panel pieces: 56 cm (22 in) wide x 26 cm (10¼ in) long – place corner pattern piece for top panel on the bottom edge

◤ 2 x bottom panel pieces: 51 cm (20 in) wide x 12 cm (4¾ in) long – place corner pattern piece for bottom panel on the bottom edge

◢ 2 x lining pieces: 56 cm (22 in) wide x 37 cm (14½ in) long – place corner pattern piece for lining on the bottom edge

◢ 2 x interfacing pieces: 56 cm (22 in) wide x 37 cm (14½ in) long – place corner piece for lining on the bottom edge

▶ 1 x base fabric piece: cut on the fold from base pattern piece

◢ 1 x base interfacing piece: cut on the fold from base pattern piece

◢ 1 x base lining piece: cut on the fold from base pattern piece

▶ 2 x straps: 8 cm (3 in) wide x 62 cm (24½ in) long

SEW

Bag

▶ **1** With right sides facing, align the bottom of each top panel piece with the top of a bottom panel piece. Pin together and stitch. Press the seam open.

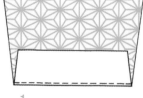

1

◢ **2** Place the bag panels together with right sides facing. Sandwich the bag panels between the two bag interfacing pieces. Pin all layers together. Stitch along both sides.

3 Stay stitch the base interfacing piece to the wrong side of the base fabric piece, 5 mm (¼ in) from the edge. With right sides facing, pin this to the bottom raw edge of the bag – the curved edges can make this a little tricky, so align the centre of each end and each side first.

4 Stitch around the edge of the entire base 5 mm (¼ in) from the edge.

4

Lining

1 Pin the lining pieces together with right sides facing. Stitch along the sides, leaving a 15 cm (6 in) opening on one side for turning the bag right side out later on.

2 Position the base lining piece as you did in step 3 for the bag and stitch on.

Straps

1 To make the straps, follow the instructions on page 15.

Assemble

1 Turn the lining right side out. On both sides of the lining, position the straps 13 cm (5 in) in from each edge, aligning the raw edges and making sure the straps are facing down to the bottom of the bag. Stitch them on, about 5 mm (¼ in) from the raw edges.

2 Turn the lining inside out. With the bag facing right side out, insert it into the lining. Make sure the handles are still facing down towards the bottom of the bag.

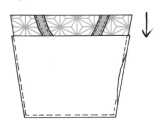

2

3 Pin the top raw edges of the bag and lining together. Stitch all the way around the top edge.

4 Pull the bag through the opening in the lining, then stitch the hole closed and push the lining down into the bag.

5 Press the top edge of the bag flat and topstitch close to the seam.

WINE BOTTLE
TOTE

With this reusable waterproof bottle tote, carrying your wine in a drab brown paper bag can be a thing of the past.

I chose oilcloth for this project for its waterproof qualities and its stability. However, oilcloth can be quite difficult to work with because of its stiff and slippery nature – you can easily substitute a heavyweight cloth such as upholstery fabric or canvas if you prefer. (If you choose to work with oilcloth, refer to the tips on page 11 before you start.)

Materials

Oilcloth or heavyweight fabric: approx. 60 cm (23⅜ in) wide x 50 cm (19¾ in) long

2.5 cm (1 in) binding, webbing or ribbon for handles and edging: 125 cm (49¼ in) long

Wine Bottle Tote base pattern piece

WINE BOTTLE TOTE

FINISHED SIZE

- 31 cm (12¼ in) wide x 27 cm (10½ in) high

CUT

- 1 x bag piece: 28.5 cm (11¼ in) wide x 35 cm (13¾ in) long
- 1 x base piece: cut from pattern piece
- 2 x webbing edging strips: 28.5 cm (11¼ in) long
- 2 x webbing handles: 33 cm (13 in) long

SEW

1 Position the handles, right side facing down, on the wrong side of the bag fabric, with the handles facing down towards the bottom of the fabric. They should be 2.5 cm (1 in) in from each side and 2.5 cm (1 in) from the top. Make sure the gap between each handle measures 4.5 cm (1¾ in). Secure the handles with small pieces of adhesive tape if you are using oilcloth.

2 Fold the top edge of the bag piece over 2.5 cm (1 in) to the wrong side of the fabric and press flat with your finger. Fold the handles up towards the top edge and secure in place with a few pieces of tape. Stitch the hem down, sewing 5 mm (¼ in) from the raw edge.

3 On the right side of the bag piece, align an edging strip to the top edge of the bag, with right side facing up. Secure in place with a few bits of tape along each edge, then stitch very close to the top and bottom edges of the webbing.

4 Measure 1 cm (⅜ in) from the bottom of your bag piece, and stitch on the second edging strip as in step 3.

1

2

4

5

7

5 Fold the bag piece in half lengthwise, with right sides facing. Stitch together along the long edge using a 1.5 cm (⅝ in) seam.

6 Make some slits around the bottom edge of the bag, to make stitching the base on easier – be careful not to cut through the stitching.

7 Position the base piece at the bottom of the bag, underneath the tabs and with wrong side facing out. Secure with some small pieces of tape. Stitch the base to the sides – this is quite fiddly, so take your time, carefully manoeuvring the fabric around as you go.

8 Turn the bag right side out – this is also fiddly as oilcloth is quite stiff, so push the bottom through first and feed the rest through gradually.

CRAFT TOTE

With room for your craft supplies as well as the things you usually cart around in your handbag, this is the perfect tote for the crafter on the move. Each of the pockets (three on the outside and two large pockets inside) has been designed with specific items in mind: knitting needles, patterns, books, and tools such a scissors and pins. The Craft Tote is extra large and sturdy, and doubles as a storage place for your projects.

As an alternative to leather stitch-on handles, you could use webbing or make your own handles from coordinating fabric (see instructions on page 15).

Materials

- Medium–heavy weight cotton fabric for bag, side panels and base: approx. 115 cm (45¼ in) wide x 150 cm (59 in) long
- Cotton fabric for lining: approx. 115 cm (45¼ in) wide x 150 cm (59 in) long
- Cotton fabric for top outside pocket: approx. 50 cm (19¾ in) wide x 70 cm (27½ in) long
- Cotton fabric for bottom outside pocket: approx. 50 cm (19¾ in) wide x 50 cm (19¾ in) long
- Cotton fabric for knitting-needle outside pocket: approx. 20 cm (8 in) wide x 115 cm (45¼ in) long
- Heavyweight fusible interfacing: approx. 115 cm (45¼ in) wide x 150 cm (59 in) long
- Leather stitch-on handles

CRAFT TOTE

FINISHED SIZE

- 39 cm (15⅜ in) wide x 32 cm (12½ in) high

CUT

- 2 x bag pieces: 42 cm (16½ in) wide x 37 cm (14½ in) long
- 2 x side panel pieces: 15 cm (6 in) wide x 37 cm (14½ in) long
- 1 x base piece: 15 cm (6 in) wide x 42 cm (16½ in) long
- 2 x lining bag pieces: 42 cm (16½ in) wide x 37 cm (14½ in) long
- 1 x lining base piece: 15 cm (6 in) wide x 42 cm (16½ in) long
- 1 x lining pocket piece: 42 cm (16½ in) wide x 54 cm (21¼ in) long
- 1 x large outside pocket piece: 30 cm (12 in) wide x 52 cm (20½ in) long
- 1 x small outside pocket piece: 30 cm (12 in) wide x 28 cm (11 in) long
- 1 x knitting-needle outside pocket piece: 15 cm (6 in) wide x 52 cm (20½ in) long
- 2 x bag interfacing pieces: 42 cm (16½ in) wide x 37 cm (14½ in) long
- 2 x side panel interfacing pieces: 15 cm (6 in) wide x 37 cm (14½ in) long
- 1 x base interfacing piece: 15 cm (6 in) wide x 42 cm (16½ in) long

SEW

Interfacing

1 Iron interfacing onto the bag pieces, side panels and base piece.

Pocket panel

1 Fold each outside pocket piece in half crosswise, right sides out, and press.

2 Place the small pocket piece on top of the large pocket piece, with bottom raw edges aligned. Pin in place.

3 Place the knitting-needle pocket piece on top of the large and small pocket pieces you just pinned together, right sides facing, aligning the top and right edges. Pin in place, then stitch along the right side edge. Press seam open.

3

4 Pin the pocket panel to one bag piece, both with right sides facing up and with bottom edges aligned.

5 Stitch along the seam between the wider pocket panel and the knitting-needle pocket.

5

Bag

1 Lay the bag piece with pocket panel attached right side up. Place each side panel right side down on top of the bag piece, aligning the edges. Pin, then stitch along the side edges.

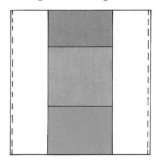

1

2 With right sides facing, align the raw side edges of the side panels with the other bag piece and stitch together.

3 With right sides facing, align the bottom edges of the bag and side panels with the base piece, and stitch together. Turn right side out.

Lining

1 Fold the lining pocket piece in half with wrong sides facing so it measures 42 cm (16½ in) wide x 27 cm (10⅝ in) long, and press. Stitch across the folded edge, close to the fold.

2 Place the pocket piece on top of one lining piece, with right sides of both facing up, aligning the side and bottom edges. Stitch along the sides.

3 Measure 21 cm (8¼ in) across the pocket piece to find the centre and draw a vertical line. Stitch down the centre of the pocket piece to divide the pocket in two.

4 Assemble the lining following the steps for sewing the bag pieces together (above), but leave an opening of about 20 cm (8 in) in one side seam of the lining for turning right side out.

Assemble

1 With the bag right side out and the lining wrong side out, insert the bag into the lining.

2 Pin the top raw edges of the bag and lining together. Stitch all the way around the top edge.

3 Pull the bag through the opening in the lining. (Do not stitch the opening closed yet.)

4 Press the top edge of the bag flat and topstitch close to the seam.

5 Position the handles on your bag where you think they look best (depending on what sort of handles you are using). Reaching in through the opening in the lining, stitch the handles onto the bag. (Don't stitch through the lining.)

6 When the bag handles are secured in place, close the opening in the lining, then push the lining down into the bag.

HANDLEBAR LUNCH TOTE

Pack your lunch in this colourful tote and use the velcro straps to attach it to the handlebars on your pushbike. Tuck the handles inside the bag while it's attached to your bike, then pull them out when you reach your destination to carry the bag as a regular lunch tote.

Made from Mexican oilcloth, which is waterproof and easy to clean, this compact lunch tote is not only pretty but also very practical. (Read the tips on working with oilcloth on page 11 before you begin.)

If you're not much of a cyclist, simply leave the velcro straps off the back of the bag and use it as a regular lunch tote instead.

Materials

- Mexican oilcloth: approx. 120 cm (47¼ in) wide x 50 cm (19¾ in) long
- Velcro (hook-and-loop tape) for straps: approx. 40 cm (15¾ in) long
- 2.5 cm (1 in) webbing for straps and handles: approx. 2 cm (2¼ yd) long
- Leather needle
- Pinking shears (if you want zigzag edges)

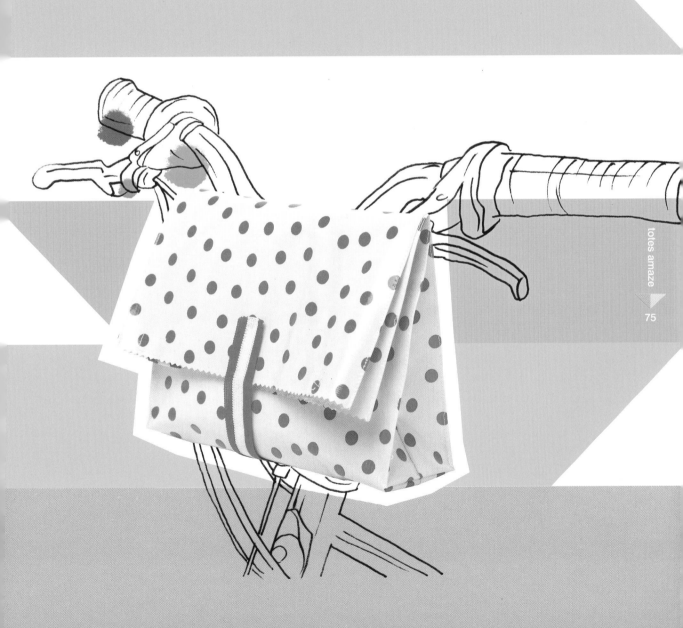

HANDLEBAR LUNCH TOTE

FINISHED SIZE

- 23 cm (9 in) wide x 32 cm (12⅝ in) high

CUT

- 2 x bag pieces: 33 cm (13 in) wide x 37 cm (14½ in) long (cut the top edges with pinking shears if desired)
- 3 x velcro strips (both the hook and loop sides): 13 cm (5 in) long
- 3 x webbing straps: 26 cm (10¼ in) long (seal the cut ends with fray-stop or clear nail polish, or overlock/zigzag stitch to prevent fraying)
- 2 x webbing handles: 60 cm (23¾ in) long (seal the ends as above)

SEW

Straps

1 Take two of the 26 cm (10¼ in) webbing straps and, on the wrong side of each, sew a 13 cm (5 in) strip of hook tape to the bottom end of the strap, stitching close to the edges. Then stitch the matching strip of loop tape to the top end of the strap.

2 On the right side of the back bag piece (remembering that the top half of this will fold over to the front of the bag), measure 6 cm (2⅜ in) from the bottom and 7 cm (2¾ in) in from each side, and position the webbing straps. Hold in place with some small pieces of tape, then stitch only the bottom half of each strap to the bag piece.

3 Measure 16.5 cm (6½ in) from the sides of the bag and stitch on the remaining 13 cm (5 in) strip of velcro hook tape between the two straps.

1

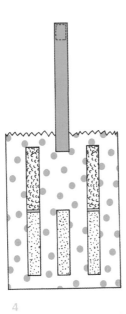

4

4 Trim the remaining 13 cm (5 in) strip of loop tape to 5 cm (2 in) and sew onto the bottom end of the remaining 26 cm (10¼ in) strap of webbing. Measure 16.5 cm (6½ in) across the top of the bag and 3 cm (1¼ in) down from the top edge, and make a mark. Stitch on the top end of the strap of webbing – this will wrap around and match up with the velcro hook tape on the back of the bag.

Handles

1 Lay each bag piece wrong side up and position the handles 7 cm (2¾ in) in from each side edge and 2 cm (¾ in) from the top. Stitch on.

Bag

1 Place the bag pieces together with right sides facing, and stitch along the sides and across the bottom.

2 To create the boxed corners, follow the instructions on page 14, measuring 4 cm (1½ in) from the corner point.

3 Turn the bag right side out and topstitch along each of the four side folds.

3

RECYCLED COFFEE SACK TOTE

This tote is made using a recycled coffee sack for the front of the bag only. You can use the sack fabric for the back of the bag too if you like, just remember to add another piece of lining as backing for this piece.

There's something quite satisfying about being able to reuse fabric that would otherwise be discarded. Hessian coffee sacks are widely used to transport coffee beans and can usually be found at your local coffee house for a song. The designs printed on them are quite varied and exotic, and as an added bonus the material still has a faint aroma of coffee.

Materials

- Hessian (burlap) coffee sack for bag front
- Light–medium weight cotton or canvas fabric for bag back: approx. 60 cm (23⅝ in) wide x 70 cm (27½ in) long
- Light–medium weight cotton fabric for lining and pocket: approx. 115 cm (45¼ in) wide x 150 cm (59 in) long
- Heavy interfacing: approx. 115 cm (45¼ in) wide x 70 cm (27½ in) long – if you can't find heavy interfacing at your local craft store, use two layers of mediumweight interfacing
- Braided webbing for handles and strap: 180 cm (71 in) long – available online, by the metre

RECYCLED COFFEE SACK TOTE

FINISHED SIZE

- 45 cm (17¾ in) wide x 36 cm (14¼ in) high

CUT

- 1x bag front piece: 44 cm (17⅜ in) wide x 49 cm (19¼ in) long

- 1 x bag back piece: 44 cm (17⅜ in) wide x 49 cm (19¼ in) long

- 3 x lining pieces (one for backing the hessian): 44 cm (17⅜ in) wide x 49 cm (19¼ in) long

- 2 x interfacing pieces: 44 cm (17⅜ in) x 49 cm (19¼ in)

- 1 x pocket piece: 19 cm (7½ in) x 17.5 cm (7 in)

- 2 x webbing handles: 52 cm (20½ in) long

- 1 x webbing strap: 73 cm (28¾ in) long

SEW

Bag

1 Place the front bag piece on top of the back bag piece, right sides facing together. Place the extra backing piece of lining on top. Sandwich these three pieces between the two pieces of interfacing. Pin all layers together. Stitch along both sides and across the bottom.

2 To create the boxed corners, follow the instructions on page 14, measuring 6 cm (2⅜ in) from the corner point. Turn the bag right side out. (If you feel that the base isn't sturdy enough, turn the bag inside out again, cut a piece of fusible interfacing to the size of the base and iron it on.)

Pocket

1 To create the hemmed edge pocket, follow the instructions on page 17.

Lining

1 On the right side of one of the lining pieces, position the pocket 9 cm (3½ in) from the top edge and 15.5 cm (6 in) from each side. Stitch along the sides and across the bottom, close to the edge.

2 Pin the lining pieces together with right sides facing. Stitch along both sides and across the bottom, leaving a 15 cm (6 in) opening on one side seam for turning the bag right side out later on.

3 Create boxed corners for the lining, as in step 2 for sewing the bag.

Handles and strap

1 On both sides of the lining (right sides facing out), position the handles 13 cm (5 in) in from each edge, aligning the raw edges. Make sure the handles are facing down to the bottom of the bag. Stitch them on, about 5 mm (¼ in) from the raw edges.

2 Position the long strap on the centre of the side fold on both sides of the lining, aligning the raw edges. Stitch it on, about 5 mm (¼ in) from the raw edges.

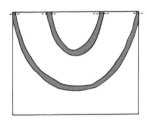

2

Assemble

1 Turn the lining inside out. With the bag facing right side out, insert it into the lining. Make sure the handles are facing towards the bottom of the bag.

2 Pin the top raw edges of the bag and lining together. Stitch all the way around the top edge.

3 Pull the bag through the opening in the lining, then stitch the hole closed and push the lining down into the bag.

4 Press the top edge of the bag flat, using a cotton pressing cloth to protect the hessian and handles.

5 Topstitch around the top edge of the bag (because of the thickness of the webbing, you may have to stitch to the edge of each strap but not over it to avoid a broken needle).

TIPS

It's not advisable to wash hessian coffee sacks, as the dye on the print will run and the hessian will fray (I learnt this the hard way!). Airing the sack out on the clothesline is the best way to remove the coffee smell.

Hessian has a loose weave and looks best with a backing applied between the hessian and the lining – this will also give more structure to the bag. Cut an extra piece of lining if using a beige or natural-coloured fabric, or back the lining with light-coloured interfacing.

Hessian is prone to fraying, so care is required when cutting and sewing near the cut edges. The fibres will end up all over you and your workspace, so don't wear your Sunday best when working with hessian!

If the coffee sack is really creased, it can be ironed on the reverse side with a dry iron, using a pressing cloth to protect the fabric.

REVERSIBLE TOTE

This cute little tote has four distinct features that make it wonderfully customisable: pleats, a detachable fabric bloom, clip-on handles and reversibility.

Clip-on handles are much stronger than they look, yet are easily removed when you want to reverse the bag or swap them for a different set of handles. If you prefer, you could use webbing handles – just keep in mind that the handles need to look good from both sides if you want the bag to be reversible.

The fabric bloom can be attached to either side of the bag. Make it in matching or contrasting fabric, or a combination of both. It's the perfect way to use up any scrap fabric.

Materials

- Cotton fabric for bag: approx. 115 cm (45¼ in) wide x 60 cm (23⅝ in) long
- Cotton fabric for lining: approx. 115 cm (45¼ in) x 60 cm (23½ in) long
- Cotton fabric for bloom: use offcuts from the bag/lining
- 2 cm (¾ in) bias binding: 1 m (39 in) long – use ready-made binding, or make your own (see instructions on page 19)
- Clip-on handles – available online
- Reversible Tote pattern pieces: bag; blooms

REVERSIBLE TOTE

FINISHED SIZE

▶ 45 cm (17¾ in) wide x 32 cm (12⅝ in) high

CUT

▶ 2 x bag pieces: cut on the fold from bag pattern piece

◢ 2 x lining pieces: cut on the fold from bag pattern piece

▶ 2 x bloom pieces in each size: cut from pattern pieces

◢ 2 x bias binding strips: 20 cm (8 in) long

▶ 2 x bias binding strips: 28 cm (11 in) long

SEW

Fabric bloom

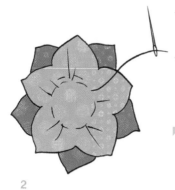

▶ **1** Stack all the bloom pieces on top of each other, right sides facing up, alternating the petal position. Make sure the larger pieces are at the bottom and the smallest pieces are on top.

◢ **2** Hand stitch these pieces together using a simple running stitch, pulling the layers together as you go.

▶ **3** Attach a safety pin to the back of the bloom, or cut a small circle of felt and sew this to the back of the bloom, then stitch a brooch pin to the felt.

▶ **4** Cover a button with the same fabric or find a lovely old vintage button and stitch it to the centre of the bloom if you wish. You could also add ribbon or lace to hang down from the back of the bloom for a little something extra.

Bag

▶ **1** On each bag piece and lining piece, make four pleats along the top edge, each measuring 2 cm (¾ in). Fold the pleats on the left side of the bag towards the left, and on the right side of the bag towards the right.

2

Bag – cont.

Position the pleats so that they finish about 3.5 cm (1⅜ in) from each side of the bag and are approximately the same distance apart. (It's not essential to get measurements precise here. The key thing to remember once you have the pleats in position is to make sure that the front and back pieces match up.) Pin the pleats in place and press, then baste.

2

2 Pin the bag pieces together with right sides facing. Stitch around the bottom curved edge. Repeat with the lining fabric pieces.

3 Notch the curves on the bag and lining pieces (see page 14). Turn the bag right side out (leave the lining facing wrong side out).

Assemble

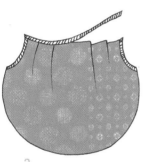

2

1 Insert the lining (still wrong side out) into the bag. Match up the raw top edges, pin, and baste in place.

2 To apply the bias binding, follow the instructions on page 19. Apply the two shorter pieces of binding to the side edges of the bag, then the two longer pieces to the top edges on the front and back of the bag.

3 Choose which side will be the outside of your bag (at least for today!) and clip on the handles and fabric bloom.

3

PAINT-YOUR-OWN TOTES

Do you have a boring old calico tote that needs a bit of pizazz? Whip out some paints and start decorating! You don't have to be an artist to create a unique tote: find household objects for stencils, carve up a potato stamp, or simply use some masking tape to create your design. The options are only limited by your imagination.

These projects are very simple and require very few materials. Fabric paints, masking tape, and a few potatoes will provide endless design possibilities.

Materials

You'll find an itemised list of materials needed for each project over the page.

- Calico tote
- Fabric dye
- Sink or bucket
- Coat hanger
- Timer
- Fabric paint
- Stamp made from sponge or potato, or a round stencil
- Masking tape
- Paint brush
- Piece of lace
- Spray adhesive

- Fabric spray paint.
- A good-sized potato
- Small sharp knife or cookie cutter
- Paper towel
- Scrap paper
- Royalty-free clip-art silhouettes
- Printer
- Iron-on transfer paper
- Iron
- Cotton pressing cloth

PAINT-YOUR-OWN TOTES

DIP-DYED TOTE

It's a trend for good reason. Dip-dyeing is not only easy but looks great too. Here's a quick guide to dip-dyeing. You'll need: calico tote, dye, sink or bucket, coathanger.

1 Wet your tote and squeeze out the excess water.

2 Mix the dye to desired strength (follow the instructions on the packet or bottle).

3 Attach the tote to the coat hanger, making sure that the handles are tied up and out of the way (you want to avoid dyeing those too!).

4 Stick a pin in each side of the bag where you want the dye to stop.

5 Immerse the tote in the dye up to the pins for 1 minute, then gradually pull it out of the dye about 5 cm (2 in). Leave for 5 minutes more. Continue pulling the bag out a little at a time, increasing the waiting period by 5 minutes each time. The dye will seep up the tote, creating a nice graded effect. When you get to the bottom of the bag, if you feel that it needs to be darker, simply immerse it for a little longer. The trick is to hold the tote straight as you go, so that the grading looks even.

6 When you're satisfied with the look of your dye, rinse out the excess and set the colour according to the instructions and hang the bag to dry. Note that some of the dye may still come out when you wash the bag, so it's best to hand wash it or avoid putting it in the machine with lighter colours.

SPOTTY TOTE

Spots never go out of style, and the possibilities are endless. Big spots, small spots – choose fabric paints or pens in colours that make you happy and get spotting! Spot freehand, find a circle around the house that you can use as a stencil, make a potato stamp, or blot spots on with a sponge.

STRIPED TOTE

It doesn't get any simpler than this. All you need is masking tape and one colour of fabric paint. Make one horizontal stripe or many, or go crazy and run the stripes diagonally or vertically. Make the distance between each strip of tape less and less for a graded effect; or stick the tape down at random angles to create a geometric design, filling each shape in with a different colour. You'll need: calico tote, masking tape, fabric paint, paint brush.

1 Arrange masking tape on your tote in the design of your choice – be sure to press the edges of the tape flat to create a nice sharp line.

2 Paint the surface of the bag with one colour or many, depending on your design.

3 Once the paint has dried, carefully peel back the masking tape.

STENCILLED TOTE

Create a design, trace it and cut it out of stencil film, then paint your unique work of art onto your tote. If that sounds too complicated, simply find a stencil you love and use that instead. Be on the lookout for things around the house that could work as a stencil, or rummage through your local charity store for old lace curtains, tablecloths or doilies.

Here's how to use a lace stencil. Lace with larger holes will create a bold design, while a fine lace will be more subtle once painted. You'll need: calico tote, some lace, spray adhesive, fabric spray paint.

1 Cut out a section of lace. Spray one side with a light layer of spray adhesive. Gently stick the lace to the tote.

2 Spray paint over the lace to fill all the holes.

3 Carefully pull up the lace before it sticks for good, and admire your lacy handiwork.

POTATO STAMP TOTE

The humble potato: not only is it delicious, it also makes a great stamp for fabric printing. You'll need: calico tote, a good-sized potato, small sharp knife or cookie cutter, paper towel, scrap paper, fabric paint, paint brush.

1 Slice the potato in half and carve your design into it, or use a cookie cutter for cutting letters or shapes. (You can cut letters out of multiple potatoes, then thread them on to a skewer to create a word.)

2 Blot the potato stamp on paper towel to dry the surface, then brush a thin layer of paint onto it and press evenly over the fabric. (Do a test on paper first to get a feel for the paint thickness and how much pressure to apply.)

IRON-ON TRANSFER SILHOUETTES

Find some royalty-free clip-art silhouettes, print them using iron-on transfer paper and iron them on to your tote. Follow the instructions on the transfer paper package to ensure perfect results.

TIE TOTE

Just tie a different pretty bow around this simple tote to change the look each time you use it. Coordinate with your outfit by selecting fabric in complementary colours.

A medium-sized bag for carrying your everyday essentials, the Tie Tote is very versatile in its proportions, shape and style.

The instructions don't include a pocket or magnetic snap closure, but it's a cinch to add these if you wish (see pages 15-18).

Materials

- Medium–heavy weight cotton fabric for bag and straps: approx. 115 cm (45¼ in) wide x 90 cm (35½ in) long
- Lightweight cotton fabric for lining: approx. 115 cm (45¼ in) wide x 60 cm (23⅝ in) long
- Fabric for tie: approx. 115 cm (45¼ in) wide x 50 cm (19¾ in) long
- Tie Tote corner pattern piece

TIE TOTE

FINISHED SIZE

➤ 43 cm (17 in) wide x 35 cm
(13¾ in) high

CUT

* Refer to instructions on page 8
for placing and cutting corner
pieces.

▸ 2 x bag pieces: 46 cm (18 in)
wide x 37 cm (14½ in) long –
place corner pattern piece on
the bottom edge

◂ 2 x lining pieces: 46 cm (18 in)
wide x 37 cm (14½ in) long –
place corner pattern piece on
the bottom edge

➤ 2 x straps: 8 cm (3 in) wide x
67 cm (26⅜ in) long

◂ 2 x tie pieces: 14 cm (5½ in)
wide x 92 cm (36¼ in) long

SEW

Bag

➤ **1** Pin the bag pieces together with right
sides facing. Stitch along the sides and
across bottom. Notch the curves (see
page 14).

Lining

▸ **1** Pin the lining pieces together with right
sides facing. Stitch along the sides and
across the bottom, leaving a 15 cm
(6 in) opening on one side seam for
turning right side out later on. Notch
the curves.

Straps

◂ **1** To make the straps, follow the
instructions on page 15.

Assemble

➤ **1** With the bag right side out, insert it into
the lining (which should still be wrong
side out).

▸ **2** Pin the top raw edges of the bag
and lining together. Stitch all the way
around the top edge.

3 Pull the bag through the opening in the lining, then stitch the hole closed and push the lining down into the bag.

4 Press the top edge of the bag flat and topstitch close to the edge.

5 On both sides of the bag, position the straps 7.5 cm (3 in) in from each side and 7.5 cm (3 in) from the top edge, tucking the raw edges under by 1 cm (⅜ in). Pin in place.

6 Attach the straps, and at the same time create the loops for the tie, by sewing across the bottom of each strap close to the fold and across each strap where it meets the top edge of the bag.

Tie

1 Pin the two tie pieces together with right sides facing. Stitch together across one short side. Press this seam open.

2 Fold the joined piece in half lengthwise with right sides facing, and stitch 5 mm (¼ in) from the raw edge.

3 Press the seam open, and turn the strap right side out. (A safety pin attached to one end will make feeding the fabric through a lot easier.)

4 Press the strap flat, with the seam centred. Fold each end in at an angle, and stitch closed.

5 Feed the tie through the loops on the bag, and tie it in a bow. If you don't wish to change the tie in the future, you can stitch along the seam at the back, making sure it is centred on the bag, to secure it in place.

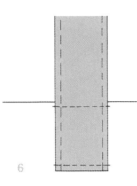

GYM TOTE

Less bounce, more pounce — what are you waiting for! Get stitching on your own individual gym tote and keep all those brand devotees wondering.

The Gym Tote has gathered external pockets, perfectly sized to fit a water bottle and other essentials. The top of the tote gathers in with a bow on each side. If you want to add some internal pockets, refer to the instructions on pages 16-18.

Materials

- Heavy weight cotton fabric for bag: approx. 115 cm (45¼ in) wide x 70 cm (27½ in) long
- Light weight cotton fabric for lining: approx. 115 cm (45¼ in) wide x 70 cm (27½ in) long
- Medium–heavy weight interfacing: approx. 115 cm (45¼ in) wide x 70 cm (27½ in) long
- Heavy weight cotton fabric for pocket: approx. 100 cm (39 in) wide x 40 cm (15¾ in) long
- 4 cm (1½ in) cotton webbing for straps, ties and pockets: 4.5 m (5 yd) long
- 1 cm (⅜ in) elastic: 50 cm (19⅝ in) long

GYM TOTE

FINISHED SIZE

▸ 40 cm (15¾ in) wide x 45 cm (17¾ in) high

CUT

▸ 2 x bag pieces: 52 cm (20½ in) wide x 53 cm (21 in) long

▸ 2 x lining pieces: 52 cm (20½ in) wide x 53 cm (21 in) long

▸ 2 x interfacing pieces: 52 cm (20½ in) wide x 53 cm (21 in) long

▸ 1 x pocket piece: 83 cm (32⅝ in) wide x 29 cm (11½ in) long

▸ 2 x webbing handles: 61 cm (24 in) long

▸ 1 x webbing strip for pocket: 83 cm (32⅝ in) long

▸ 2 x webbing ties: 115 cm (45¼ in) long

SEW

Pocket

▸ **1** Zigzag stitch or overlock the long edges of each of the bag pieces and lining pieces.

▸ **2** Fold the top edge of the pocket piece over 5 mm (¼ in) to the wrong side of the fabric and press, then fold over another 5 mm (¼ in) and stitch.

▸ **3** Align the webbing pocket strip along the top edge of the pocket piece and pin. Stitch in place, sewing very close to the top edge. Then sew along the bottom edge of the webbing to create the casing (don't sew the ends shut).

▸ **4** Mark a line 35 cm (13¾ in) along the elastic. Feed the elastic through the casing and stitch one end to the fabric. Pull the other end of the elastic through the casing until you reach the mark you made, then stitch this end down at the mark and snip off the excess.

▸ **5** Gather the fabric evenly along the elastic, then position the pocket piece right side up on the right side of one of the bag pieces.

4

7 Stretch the pocket piece out, aligning the side edges, and pin in place. (The tension created here will pull at the sides of the fabric, so you'll have to stretch it flat when sewing.)

7 Measure 14.5 cm (5¾ in) in from each side of the pocket piece and draw a vertical line. Sew two rows of stitching close together over each line to create the pocket divisions.

8 Measure 20 cm (8 in) from the top of the pocket piece and draw a horizontal line. Sew a row of stitching across to create the bottom of the pocket.

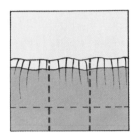

8

Bag

1 Pin the bag pieces together with right sides facing. Stitch along both sides and across the bottom, stopping 7 cm (2¾ in) from the top edge.

1

2 To create the boxed corners, follow the instructions on page 14, measuring 8 cm (3 in) from the corner point.

Lining

1 Pin the lining pieces together with right sides facing. Stitch along both sides and across the bottom, stopping 7 cm (2¾ in) from the top edge and leaving a 15 cm (6 in) opening on one side for turning right side out later on.

2 Create boxed corners for the lining, as in step 2 for sewing the bag.

Assemble

1 Turn the lining right side out. On both sides of the lining, position the handles 13 cm (5 in) in from each side edge, aligning the raw edges and making sure the handles are facing down to the bottom of the bag. Stitch them on, about 5 mm (¼ in) from the edge.

2 Turn the lining inside out. With the bag facing right side out, insert it into the lining. Make sure the handles are facing towards the bottom of the bag.

3 Pin the top raw edges of the bag and lining together. Stitch all the way around the top edge.

4 Pull the bag through the opening in the lining, then stitch the hole closed and push the lining down into the bag. Press the top edge flat.

5 Sew a horizontal line of stitching 1 cm (⅜ in) from the top edge on both sides of the bag. Then sew another row 5 cm (2 in) down from this to create the casing.

6 Feed a webbing tie strip through each side of the casing, then tie together at each side in a bow.

6

YOGA MAT TOTE

Bring your own unique style to class with this practical yet simple Yoga Mat Tote. The tote has two small ties attached to the lining to keep the mat secure and balanced while you are carrying it.

Materials

- Heavyweight cotton fabric for bag: approx. 60 cm (23⅝ in) wide x 60 cm (23⅝ in) long
- Lightweight cotton fabric for lining: approx. 60 cm (23⅝ in) wide x 60 cm (23⅝ in) long
- Mediumweight interfacing: approx. 60 cm (23⅝ in) wide x 60 cm (23⅝ in) long

- 2.5 cm (1 in) webbing for straps: 2.5 m (2¾ yd) long
- 1 cm (⅜ in) webbing for ties: 2 m (2¼ yd) long
- Yoga Mat Tote corner pattern piece

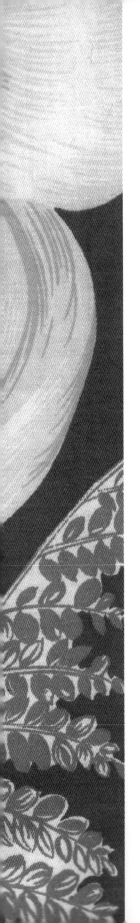

YOGA MAT TOTE

FINISHED SIZE

▶ 44.5 cm (17½ in) wide x 22 cm (8¾ in) high

CUT

▶ 1 x bag piece: 47 cm (18½ in) x 47 cm (18½ in)

◢ 1 x lining piece: 47 cm (18½ in) x 47 cm (18½ in)

▶ 1 x interfacing piece: 47 cm (18½ in) x 47 cm (18½ in)

◢ *For each of the cut fabric pieces: fold the square in half, then in half again, making sure the fabric is folded flat. Place the corner pattern piece on the raw edges (not the folded edges!). Mark the line and cut the corners off. Press the bag and lining pieces flat.

2 x 2.5 cm (1 in) webbing straps: 125 cm (49¼ in) long

2 x 1 cm (⅜ in) webbing ties for the lining: 75 cm (29½ in) long

2 x 1 cm (⅜ in) webbing ties for the top of the bag: 20 cm (8 in) long

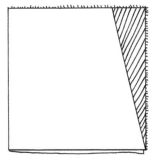

SEW

Lining

▶ **1** On the right side of the lining piece, measure 12 cm (4¾ in) in from each side across the centre, and make a mark. Stitch across the middle of the webbing ties for the lining at each of these marks. (These are the ties that will secure your mat in place.)

1

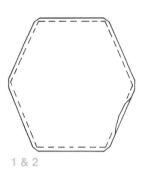

1 & 2

Bag

◤ **1** Place the bag and lining pieces together with right sides facing, then put the interfacing piece on top of the lining piece. Pin all the layers together. Sew around the edges, pivoting at each corner and leaving a 15 cm (6 in) opening on one side for turning.

◤ **2** Trim each corner (see page 14).

◤ **3** Turn right side out, press, then close the opening.

2

Straps

◤ **1** Lay the bag with the outside fabric facing up. Starting from the centre, align each webbing strap along one edge and then down the opposite side. Make sure the straps aren't twisted before pinning in place.

◤ **2** Stitch on the straps, sewing close to both edges of the webbing.

Ties

◤ **1** Measure 16.5 cm (6½ in) across the top of the bag on both sides and pin the remaining webbing ties to the lining. Turn the raw ends of the webbing under and stitch on.

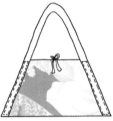

1

SIX-IN-ONE FOLDING TOTE

Six options in the one bag – you'll be spoilt for choice! Best of all, this project is very simple and takes no time to whip up. A tote, a purse and a clutch: the Six-in-one Tote is designed with the creative girl in mind. Choose two fabrics that complement each other, then simply fold the tote to suit the occasion.

Unfolded, the bag is a slouch tote roomy enough to carry all your day-to-day necessities and gadgets. Fold the top over to make a smaller shoulder bag for carrying your essentials, or tuck the strap away entirely and step out in the evening with an oversized clutch.

Materials

- Medium–heavyweight fabric for bag front: approx. 60 cm (23⅝ in) wide x 70 cm (27½ in) long
- Light weight or medium–heavyweight fabric for bag back: approx. 60 cm (23⅝ in) wide x 70 cm (27½ in) long
- Light weight cotton fabric for lining: approx. 115 cm (45¼ in) wide x 70 cm (27½ in) long
- Lightweight interfacing: approx. 115 cm (45¼ in) wide x 70 cm (27½ in) long
- 2.5 cm (1 in) bias binding: 2 m (2¼ yd) long
- Six-in-one Folding Tote corner pattern piece

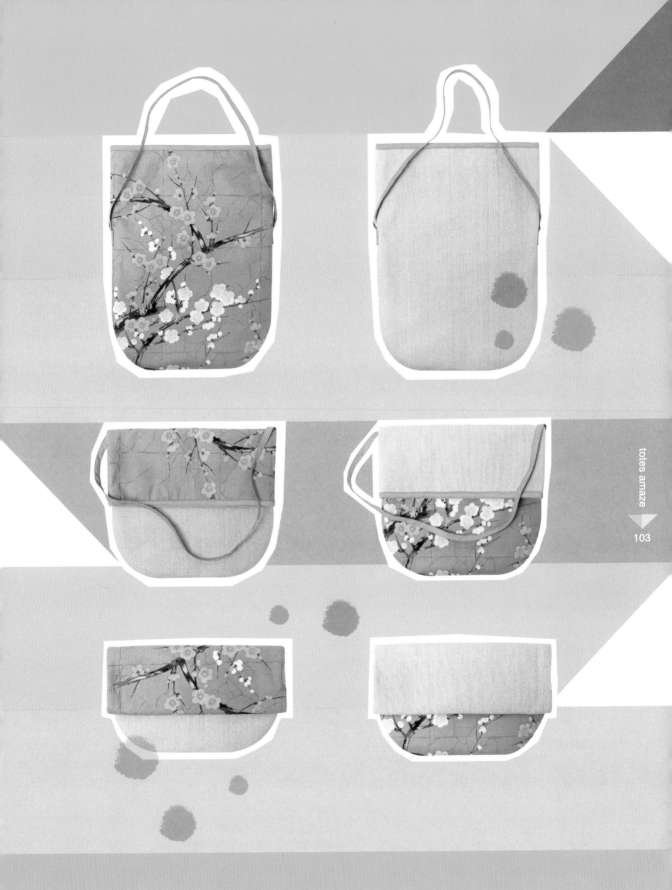

SIX-IN-ONE FOLDING TOTE

FINISHED SIZE

- Slouch tote: 34 cm (13⅜ in) wide x 45 cm (17¾ in) high
- Shoulder bag: 34 cm (13⅜ in) wide x 30 cm (12 in) high
- Clutch: 34 cm (13⅜ in) wide x 19 cm (7½ in) high

CUT

* Place the corner pattern piece on the bottom edge of each fabric/interfacing piece. (Refer to instructions on page 8 for placing and cutting corner pieces.)

- 1 x bag front piece: 37 cm (14½ in) wide x 47 cm (18½ in) long

- 1 x bag back piece: 37 cm (14½ in) wide x 47 cm (18½ in) long

- 2 x lining pieces: 37 cm (14½ in) wide x 47 cm (18½ in) long

- 2 x interfacing pieces: 37 cm (14½ in) wide x 47 cm (18½ in) long

- 1 x strip bias binding for strap: 90 cm (1 yd) long

- 1 x strip bias binding for trim: 80 cm (31½ in) long

SEW

Bag

1 Place the bag pieces together with right sides facing. Sandwich the bag pieces between the two pieces of interfacing. Pin all layers together. Stitch along both sides and across the bottom.

2 Turn the bag right side out.

Lining

1 Pin the lining pieces together with right sides facing. Stitch along both sides and across the bottom.

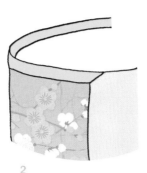

2

Strap

◢ **1** Fold the strap bias binding strip in half lengthwise and stitch along the entire length, close to each edge.

Assemble

▽ **1** Insert the lining, still wrong side out, into the bag (which is right side out). Match up the top raw edges and baste in place.

◣ **2** Following the instructions on page 19, apply the bias binding trim around the entire top edge of the bag, starting at the side seam and allowing 1 cm (⅜ in) of overlap.

◢ **3** Measure 20 cm (8 in) down from the top edge of the bag and make a mark on either side at the seam.

◣ **4** Fold each end of the strap under by 2.5 cm (1 in), then stitch the strap to the sides of the bag at the marks by sewing a rectangle across the width of the strap.

4

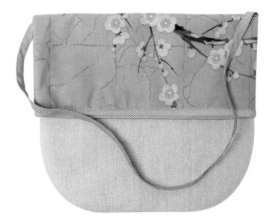

MUMS'
TOTE

Mothers: take note! Carrying all your baby bits and bobs around in style need not be an overly complicated task. A few hours and some pretty fabric can make you the envy of all the mums at your local park or cafe. This tote is not only limited to mums of course – anyone who has a need for ample space and lots of pockets will love this bag.

This shapely tote has three large pockets inside. Three more pockets can easily be added by cutting an extra pocket piece using the pattern and adding it to the inside or outside of the bag. Adapt the bag to suit your own individual needs.

Materials

- Cotton fabric for bag: approx. 115 cm (45¼ in) wide x 80 cm (31½ in) long
- Cotton fabric for lining: approx. 115 cm (45¼ in) wide x 120 cm (47¼ in) long
- Lightweight interfacing: approx. 115 cm (45¼ in) wide x 80 cm (31½ in) long
- 2.5 cm (1 in) webbing or braid for straps: 46 cm (18 in) long
- Magnetic bag snap
- Mums' Tote pattern pieces: bag; pocket

MUMS' TOTE

FINISHED SIZE

- 48 cm (19 in) wide x 34 cm (13⅜ in) high

CUT

- 2 x bag pieces: cut on the fold from bag pattern piece (transfer dart and magnetic snap markings)

- 2 x lining pieces: cut on the fold from bag pattern piece

- 2 x interfacing pieces: cut on the fold from bag pattern piece

- 1 x pocket piece (or more if you want more than three pockets): cut on the fold from pocket pattern piece

- 2 x webbing/braid straps: 23 cm (9 in) long

SEW

Pocket

1 Turn the top edge of the pocket piece over 5 mm (¼ in) to the wrong side of the fabric and press, then turn over another 5 mm (¼ in) and pin in place. Stitch along the folded edge, close to the fold.

Bag

1 Pin an interfacing piece to the wrong side of each bag piece and baste in place.

2 To make the darts on each bag piece, follow the instructions on page 13.

3 Pin the bag pieces together with right sides facing. Stitch around the body edge only, stopping where the handles begin.

4 Notch the curves (see page 14).

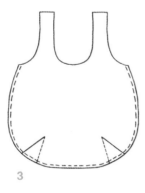

3

Lining

1 To attach the magnetic snap to the lining pieces, follow the instructions on page 15.

2 Make the darts on each lining piece, as in step 2 for sewing the bag.

3 Place the pocket piece right side up on top of one of the lining pieces, also right side up, and pin in place. Trim the excess from the edges of the pocket piece where it doesn't match up with the lining piece at the curves (this is necessary because of the shaping created by the darts). Baste in place.

4 To divide the pocket into three sections, measure 16 cm (6¼ in) in from each side and draw a vertical line. Stitch along each line.

4

5 Pin the lining pieces together with right sides facing. Stitch around the body edge only, leaving a 10 cm (4 in) opening in the bottom for turning right side out later on.

6 Notch the curves (see page 14).

Assemble

1 With the bag right side out and the lining still wrong side out, insert the bag into the lining.

2 Pin the top raw edges of the bag and lining together. Stitch around the handles and top edge, leaving the ends of the handles open.

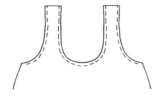

2

3 Pull the bag through the opening in the lining, pushing the handles through with a pen or knitting needle. Stitch the hole closed, then push the lining down into the bag. Press the edges flat.

4 Fold the handle ends over 1 cm (⅜ in) to the inside and press.

5 Insert the ends of the straps 1.5 cm (⅝ in) into each handle end and stitch across the handles to secure. (Be sure to insert each strap into handles on the same side of the bag, not into the handles opposite each other.)

5

6 Topstitch around the handles and top edge of the bag, close to the folded seam.

BALLOON TOTE

Soar to lofty heights with this bucket-style tote, which takes its inspiration from colourful hot air balloons.

These instructions are for a simple, unlined, round-based tote. You can add a lining and internal pockets if you like, or perhaps a large pocket on the outside of the bag.

Pompoms and tassels add a little extra playfulness to this drawstring bag. Add more or fewer, in contrasting or complementary colours, to suit your individual style.

Materials

- ▲ Medium–heavy weight cotton fabric: approx. 150 cm (59 in) wide x 100 cm (39 in) long
- ▲ Cord for drawstring: 120 cm (47¼ in) long
- ▲ Tassels and/or pompoms (see instructions for making your own on page 20)
- ▲ Balloon Tote base pattern piece

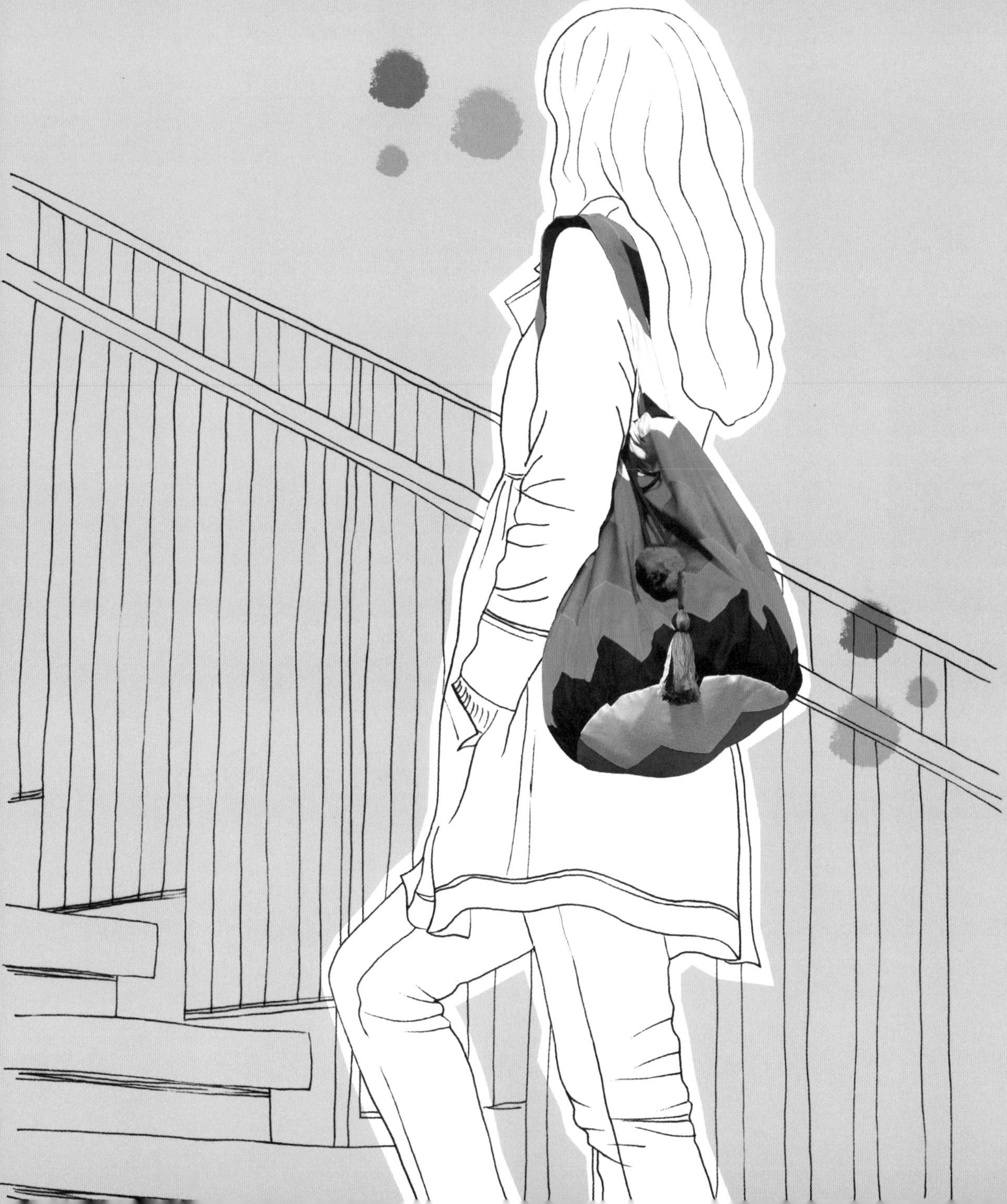

BALLOON TOTE

FINISHED SIZE

- 40 cm (15¾ in) wide x 38 cm (15 in) high

CUT

- 1 x bag piece: 44 cm (17¼ in) high x 60 cm (23⅝ in) wide, cut on the fold – so the opened piece measures 44 cm (17¼ in) x 120 cm (47¼ in)
- 1 x base piece: cut from pattern
- 2 x strap pieces: 8 cm (3 in) wide x 60 cm (23⅝ in) long

SEW

Bag

1 Zigzag stitch or overlock the short raw edges of the bag piece.

2 On the wrong side of the bag piece, measure 4.5 cm (1¾ in) from the top (long) raw edge and draw a horizontal line across. Draw another horizontal line 3.5 cm (1⅜ in) down from this line.

3

3 Fold the top edge of the bag piece over 5 mm (¼ in) to the wrong side of the fabric and press. Then turn the top edge over again to meet the second line (the fold should be on the first line), press and pin in place. To create the casing, sew a line of stitching 5 mm (¼ in) from the top and bottom edges of this fold.

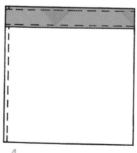

4

4 Fold the bag piece in half with right sides facing and stitch along the side edge, without stitching over the casing. Press the seam open.

5 Set your sewing machine to the longest stitch length and sew two rows of stitching, about 5 mm (¼ in) apart, close to the bottom raw edge of the bag. Don't backstitch to secure the thread, and leave a length of thread at each end of the rows of stitching. Gently pull the ends of each thread, gathering the fabric along the thread as you go.

5

6 Match the base piece up with the gathered edge of the bag piece, right sides facing, and pin. (It may take a little while to get the gathering to sit just right and a bit of adjusting will be required. I suggest placing a few pins around the base to start with, and adjusting from there.)

7 Once you have the base pinned in place, stitch it onto the bag. Overlock or zigzag stitch the raw edges to prevent fraying.

7

Straps

1 To make the straps, follow the instructions on page 15 (steps 1–3 only).

2 Overlock or zigzag stitch the raw ends of the straps.

Assemble

1 Lay the bag flat with right side facing out and with the side seam in the centre. Mark 10 cm (4 in) on either side of the seam, just below the casing. Pin the ends of one strap to these marks, tucking the ends under by 1 cm (⅜ in). Stitch on at each end by sewing a square across the width of the strap, making sure you stop just below the casing.

1

2 Sew the other strap to the opposite side of the bag.

3 Feed the drawstring cord through the casing. Knot each end of the cord, then attach pompoms or tassels (or both) to the ends using a few stitches through the knot.

THE MAN TOTE

Make your man about town a tote for all his gadgets and gear. Select neutral tones in his palette of choice, whether greens and browns, or black, blues and greys.

The Man Tote has two handles, plus a longer webbing strap with swivel hooks so the tote can be worn across the body. Two external pockets are ideal for small items such as keys and wallet. Internal pockets can be added to the lining if you'd like extra storage.

Materials

- Medium–heavy weight cotton fabric for bag: approx. 115 cm (45¼ in) wide x 60 cm (23⅝ in) long
- Lightweight cotton fabric for lining: approx. 115 cm (45¼ in) wide x 60 cm (23⅝ in) long
- Cotton fabric for pocket: approx. 50 cm (19¾ in) wide x 40 cm (15¾ in) long
- Thin leather or pleather for decorative strip: approx. 50 cm (19¾ in) wide x 20 cm (8 in) long
- Interfacing: approx. 115 cm (45¼ in) wide x 60 cm (23⅝ in) long
- 3 cm (1¼ in) webbing for straps, handles and tabs: approx. 2.6 m (3 yd) long
- 2 x 3 cm (1¼ in) D-rings
- 2 x swivel hooks with 3 cm (1¼ in) D-ring connecting part

THE MAN TOTE

FINISHED SIZE

- 35 cm (13¾ in) wide x 39 cm (15⅜ in) high

CUT

- 2 x bag pieces: 39 cm (15⅜ in) wide x 47 cm (18½ in) long
- 2 x lining pieces: 39 cm (15⅜ in) wide x 47 cm (18½ in) long
- 2 x interfacing pieces: 39 cm (15⅜ in) wide x 47 cm (18½ in) long
- 1 x pocket piece: 39 cm (15⅜ in) wide x 31 cm (12¼ in) long
- 1 x leather strip: 39 cm (15⅜ in) wide x 9 cm (3½ in) long
- 2 x webbing handles: 70 cm (27½ in)
- 1 x webbing strap: 1 m (39 in) long
- 2 x webbing tabs: 5 cm (2 in) long

SEW

Pocket

1 Fold the pocket piece in half with right sides facing, so that it measures 39 cm (15⅜ in) wide x 15.5 cm (6¼ in) long.

2 Stitch together along the long side, 5 mm (¼ in) from the raw edge.

3 Turn right side out and, with the seam in the centre, press flat. Topstitch 5 mm (¼ in) from the top and bottom folded edges.

Bag

1 On the right side of each bag piece, position the webbing handles 9.5 cm (3¾ in) in from each edge and 8 cm (3 in) down from the top edge. Stitch the handles on, sewing close to the edges to create a rectangle, then sew a square across the width of the webbing at the top, with an 'X' through the centre of it to provide reinforcement.

2 On one bag piece, lay the leather strip across the ends of the handles, 7 cm (2¾ in) from the top of the bag, matching up the side edges. Fold the top edge of the leather under if thin enough, then stitch close to the top edge all the way across.

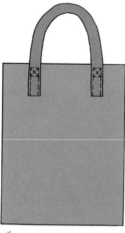

1

3 Position the pocket piece, overlapping the leather strip, 13 cm (5 in) from the top edge of the bag and pin in place. Measure 19.5 cm (7¾ in) in from one side and make a mark at the top and bottom of the pocket piece. Draw a vertical line and stitch about 2 mm (1⁄16 in) on either side of this line to create the pocket divider.

3

4 Stitch 2 mm (1⁄16 in) from the bottom edge of the pocket piece.

5 Fold each tab in half. Position the tabs on each side of the bag piece, just above the leather strip, lining up the raw edges of the tabs with the raw edges of the fabric. Insert the D-rings and pin in place.

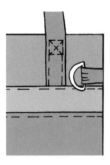

5

6 Place the bag front and back pieces together with right sides facing. Sandwich the bag pieces between the two pieces of interfacing. Pin all layers together. Stitch 1.5 cm (5⁄8 in) in from the edge along both sides and across the bottom.

7 To create the boxed corners, follow the instructions on page 14, measuring 4.5 cm (1¾ in) from the corner point. Turn the bag right side out.

Lining

1 Pin the lining pieces together with right sides facing. Stitch 1.5 cm (5⁄8 in) in from the edge along both sides and across the bottom, leaving a 15 cm (6 in) opening on one side for turning right side out later on.

2 Create boxed corners for the lining, as in step 7 for sewing the bag

Assemble

1 With the bag right side out and the handles folded down to the outside of the bag, insert the bag into the lining (which should still be wrong side out).

2 Pin the top raw edges of the bag and lining together. Stitch all the way around the top edge.

3 Pull the bag through the opening in the lining, then stitch the opening closed and push the lining down into the bag.

4 Topstitch around the top edge of the bag, close to the seam.

5 Attach the swivel hooks to the longer strap by folding the webbing over and through the hook's D-ring and stitching to secure.

6 Clip the swivel hooks to the D-rings in the tabs.

ORIGAMI TOTE

This tote is inspired by the ancient Japanese arts of origami (paper folding) and furoshiki (fabric wrapping).

The instructions are for a lined and zippered version – a zipper closes off the top of the tote and a zippered internal pocket keeps your phone and purse safe. If you find all of that a bit daunting, you can opt for a much easier version while still achieving the same look. Simply omit the lining and zippers, and hem the edges of the bag fabric instead. If you choose this option, opt for a heavier weight fabric such as canvas, denim or upholstery fabric to create structure. You can secure the top of the bag with a button if you like.

This tote uses a single square of fabric that folds over to create the bag, so I'd recommend using a plain fabric or one with a non-directional pattern.

Materials

- Cotton fabric for bag and zipper tabs: approx. 115 cm (45¼ in) wide x 100 cm (39 in) long
- Cotton fabric for lining and pocket: approx. 115 cm (45¼ in) wide x 100 cm (39 in) long
- 1 cm (⅜ in) bias binding: 4.5 m (5 yd) long
- Zipper for internal pocket: 18–20 cm (7–8 in) long
- Zipper for top of bag: 40 cm (15¾ in) long

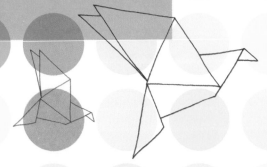

ORIGAMI TOTE

FINISHED SIZE

- 50 cm (19¾ in) wide x 30 cm (12 in) high

CUT

- 1 x bag piece: 74 cm (29 in) x 74 cm (29 in)
- 1 x lining piece 74 cm (29 in) x 74 cm (29 in)
- 1 x pocket piece: 23 cm (9 in) wide x 32 cm (12½ in) high
- 2 x zipper tab pieces: 4 cm (1½ in) x 6.5 cm (2½ in)
- 4 x strips bias binding: 104 cm (41 in) long

SEW

Pocket

1 To add an internal zippered pocket to your lining, use the instructions and measurements on page 16.

Bag

1 Pin the bag and lining pieces together with right sides facing. Stitch together, leaving a 25 cm (9¾ in) opening in the centre of the top and bottom edges. Trim the corners, then turn right side out through one of the openings and press.

1

2 Pin one side of the 40 cm (15¾ in) zipper into the top opening in the bag/lining piece, making sure it is centred, with the ends hanging out at each end. Baste in place.

3

3 On the right side of the fabric, pin a strip of bias binding (still folded in half lengthwise) along the length of this side of the square, stopping 1 cm (⅜ in) from the corners and leaving a tail of 15 cm (6 in) at each end. Stitch on the binding, close to each edge, securing the zipper in place as you go.

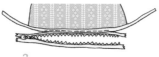

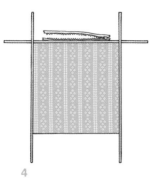

4

4 Apply binding in the same way along the two side edges without openings.

5 Lay the bag lining side up, and fold the top and bottom edges in to meet in the centre, so that the zipper you've basted in place meets up with the opening in the bottom edge of the square. Baste the second side of the zipper in place on the bottom edge, as above, then stitch a strip of binding to this edge too.

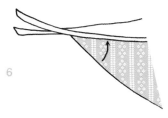

5

6 Now it's time to fold! Take the top edge and fold it to match up with the side edge. Pin these two edges together from the top corner down to where the zipper starts. Repeat this process for all four corners.

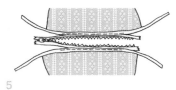

6

7 At each corner, stitch along the edge of the binding where you've pinned, sewing over the existing stitching, starting at the zipper end and continuing to the end of the tail of the binding, so that you join the two tails of binding together. Run another line of stitching along the opposite edge of the binding.

8 You will now have four tails of binding and triangular bag corners. Match up the tails of binding on each side of the bag to form the handles. Making sure the handles are not twisted, stitch them together on the wrong side, folding over the raw edges.

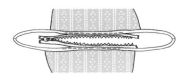

8

Zipper tabs

1 Close the zipper and centre the shorter side of one zipper tab piece over one end of the zipper with right sides facing. Stitch 5 mm (¼ in) in from the raw edge and then trim off the excess zipper length.

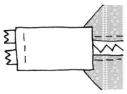

1

2 Fold the remaining three edges of the tab over 5 mm (¼ in) to the wrong side and press.

3 Fold the tab over in half, wrong sides facing, pin, and topstitch the edges.

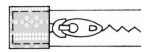

3

GLOSSARY

Back stitch To make one or two firm stitches at the beginning or end of a row of stitching to reinforce and secure. See page 10.

Baste To sew with large running stitches, or a long machine-stitch, to temporarily mark positions or to hold two or more layers of fabric together before they are permanently stitched. Also known as tacking. See page 10.

Batting See Wadding.

Bias An imaginary line at 45 degrees to the straight grain of a fabric; the bias stretches more than the straight grain (see also Grain).

Bias binding Stretchy tape made from strips of fabric cut on the bias with both long edges folded in; it may be bought or homemade. Used for binding or facing seams, hems, bag openings and the like. See pages 18-19.

Bind To finish raw edges by attaching a narrow strip of fabric (usually bias binding) that folds over to enclose the raw edge. See page 19.

Bobbin The round metal or plastic spool holding the thread that forms the underside of a machine stitch.

Casing A flat tube of fabric (created either with a double hem or an additional piece of fabric) through which cord, ribbon or elastic can be threaded, for example to draw closed the opening of a bag.

Clip To make small cuts into the seam allowance on a curved seam, so the seam will lie flat. See page 13.

Dart A triangular or diamond shaped tuck, stitched into fabric to give it a more precise shape. See page 13.

Disappearing ink marker pen An air- or water-soluble ink pen for marking fabric with stitching lines or embroidery designs (see also Dressmaker's pencil or Tailor's chalk).

Drawstring A cord or ribbon that is inserted through a hem or casing to draw up fullness or create a closure on a bag.

Dressmaker's pencil A fine chalk pencil used to mark lines on fabric. Also just called chalk pencils, they come in various colours. (See also Tailor's Chalk).

Fastener Any type of closure, such as a zipper, hook and eye, snap fastener, button, velcro or the like.

Finish To neaten a raw edge and prevent fraying by turning it under and stitching it in place, or by zigzagging, overlocking, overcasting or binding.

Gather To draw up fabric with rows of machine or hand stitching to make it narrower. See page 13.

Grain The direction of woven threads in fabric: the straight grain runs parallel to the selvedge; the opposite grain runs at right angles to the selvedge and has slightly more give than the straight grain. (See also Bias).

Hem (noun) The finished edge of a piece of fabric. (verb) To finish a raw edge by turning it under once, then usually once again, and stitching the folded edge in place by hand or by machine.

Interfacing Woven or non-woven (bonded) material used to stabilise and give body to fabric; available in a variety of weights, thicknesses and degrees of flexibility, fusible (iron-on) or sew-in forms.

Lining A separate layer of fabric attached inside a bag, used to conceal raw edges.

Needles Hand-sewing needles are made of steel with an eye at one end and a point at the other. They come in a variety of shapes and sizes, depending on their function. Machine-sewing needles have the eye near the point and a shank section that is flat on one side and fits into the needle clamp on the sewing machine.

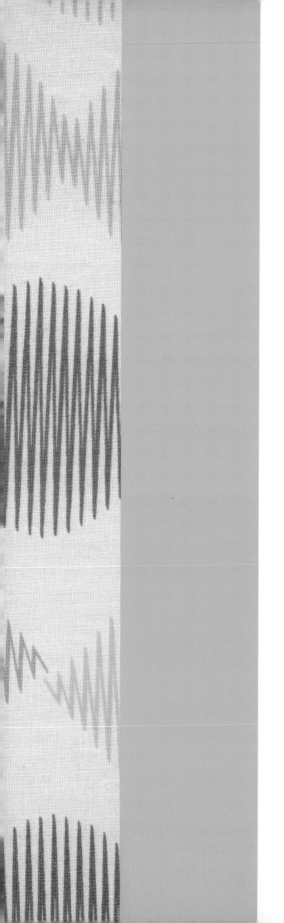

Overlock To sew, finish and simultaneously trim a seam using a specialised sewing machine known as an overlocker.

Pivot To leave the sewing machine needle in the fabric after sewing, raise the presser foot and turn the fabric to a different angle, then lower the foot and continue to sew.

Pleats Sewn-down folds in fabric, of varying widths. Pleats give fullness while reducing bulk. See page 13.

Press To use an iron. To prevent distortion and stretching during construction of a tote, the iron should not be moved back and forth as in regular ironing, but rather placed on the fabric, then lifted and moved.

Presser foot The removable part of the sewing machine that holds the fabric in place against the feed dogs when sewing.

Pressing cloth A light cotton cloth, used between the iron and delicate fabrics to protect them. You can use a clean scrap of undyed cloth, a handkerchief or even a piece of baking paper.

Raw edge The cut, unfinished edge of a piece of fabric, which can fray easily.

Seam (or Seam line) The line of hand or machine stitching joining two pieces of fabric.

Seam allowance The margin of fabric outside the stitched seam line; normally 1 cm (⅜ in) in this book, unless specified otherwise.

Seam ripper A small pointed tool with a sharp blade, used for unpicking seams or cutting stitches. Also known as an unpicker or 'quick unpick'.

Selvedge The woven edge along the sides of a width of fabric. Selvedges don't fray. However, they shrink at a greater rate than the rest of the fabric, so they should be cut off before using the fabric.

Stay-stitch To sew a line of machine stitching just inside the seam line on a curved edge to stabilise and keep the curve from distorting.

Tack See Baste.

Tailor's chalk Hard sharp-edged chalk used to make temporary markings on fabric. (See also Dressmaker's Pencil).

Tension The pressure placed on the upper and lower threads as they are fed through a sewing machine; when the tension is set perfectly, the link between the upper and lower threads is in the centre of the fabric layers.

Topstitch To make a line of hand or machine stitching (decorative or functional) on the right side of the work, at a measured distance from finished edges or seams. See page 10.

Trim To remove excess seam allowance or fabric with scissors. Also a generic term for items such as braid, ribbon, cord or lace that are used to embellish a project.

Tuck A fold or a pleat in fabric that is usually sewn in place.

Turn right side out To turn the right side of a project or section to the outside, after sewing the seams on the wrong side.

Unpicker See Seam Ripper.

Velcro The original registered trade name of nylon hook-and-loop fastener tape, now used as the generic name.

Wadding A layer of insulating material – commonly cotton, wool, polyester or a blend of these – inserted between two layers of fabric. Also known as batting.

Zigzag stitch A machine stitch that goes from side to side, producing a serrated effect; useful for finishing raw edges. See page 10.

Zipper foot A removable sewing machine foot that accommodates the teeth of a zipper on one side, making insertion easier. Special zipper feet are available for inserting invisible zippers.

RESOURCES

Alexander Henry Fabrics
www.ahfabrics.com

Anna Maria Horner
www.annamariahorner.com

BeBe Bold
www.bebebold.com

Duckcloth
www.duckcloth.com.au

eBay
www.ebay.com

Echino Textile Design
www.f-echino.com

Etsy
www.etsy.com

Funky Fabrix
www.funkyfabrix.com.au

IKEA
www.ikea.com

Joel Dewberry
www.joeldewberry.com

Kelani Fabrics
www.kelanifabric.com.au

Liberty
www.liberty.co.uk

Lincraft
www.lincraft.com.au

MacCulloch & Wallis
www.macculloch-wallis.co.uk

Material Obsession
www.materialobsession.com.au

Me Too Please
www.metooplease.com.au

Naomi Ito Textile
www.naniiro.jp

No Chintz
www.nochintz.com

Robert Kaufman
www.robertkaufman.com

Spotlight
www.spotlight.com.au

Studio Mio
www.studiomio.com.au

ABOUT THE AUTHOR

Amanda McKittrick (known to friends as 'Kitty') comes from a long line of crafters. She is a regular craft group member, occasional blogger, and loves to be surrounded at all times by craft, design, illustration, photography and collections. She is also the author of *Recycled Chic: 30 simple ways to recycle, renew and reinvent your pre-loved fashions.*

To keep up with Kitty's latest crafty adventures, head to her blog: **kittycollects.wordpress.com**

ACKNOWLEDGEMENTS

My heartfelt thanks to the dream team at Hardie Grant: Paul McNally, über-publisher; Heather Menzies, the most amazing design manager and friend; Helen Withycombe, senior editor extraordinaire; Jessica Redman, eagle-eyed editor; and Michelle Mackintosh, designer with a difference.

Special thanks to Anton (my unofficial editor-at-large), and to friends and family for love and support.

Last, but certainly not least: thank you, dear reader. May all your creations be totes amaze. x

Published in 2014 by Hardie Grant Books

Hardie Grant Books (Australia)
Ground Floor, Building 1
658 Church Street
Richmond, Victoria 3121
www.hardiegrant.com.au

Hardie Grant Books (UK)
Dudley House, North Suite
34–35 Southampton Street
London WC2E 7HF
www.hardiegrant.co.uk

A Cataloguing-in-Publication entry is available from the catalogue of the
National Library of Australia at www.nla.gov.au
Totes Amaze! 25 bags to make for every occasion
ISBN 978 1 74270 642 9

Publishing Director: Paul McNally
Project Editor: Helen Withycombe
Editor: Jessica Redman
Design Manager: Heather Menzies
Designer: Michelle Mackintosh
Typesetter: Transformer
Photographer and illustrator: Amanda McKittrick
Production: Todd Rechner

Colour reproduction by Splitting Image Colour Studio
Printed and bound in China by 1010 Printing International Limited